Divorcing Religion

A MEMOIR
AND SURVIVAL
HANDBOOK

Janice Selbie, RPC

Divorcing Religion Copyright © 2024 by Janice Selbie.

All rights reserved. No part of this publication may be reproduced, distributed or transmitted in any form or by any means, including photocopying, recording, or other electronic or mechanical methods, without the prior written permission of the publisher, except in the case of brief quotations embodied in critical reviews and certain other noncommercial uses permitted by copyright law.

Although the author and publisher have made every effort to ensure that the information in this book was correct at press time, the author and publisher do not assume and hereby disclaim any liability to any party for any loss, damage, or disruption caused by errors or omissions, whether such errors or omissions result from negligence, accident, or any other cause.

Disclaimer: This book is designed to provide general information for our readers. It is sold with the understanding that the publisher is not engaged to render any type of legal, business or any other kind of professional advice. The content of this book is the sole expression and opinion of the author, and not necessarily that of the publisher. No warranties or guarantees are expressed or implied by the author's choice to include any of the content in this volume. Neither the publisher nor the author shall be liable for any physical, psychological, emotional, financial, or commercial damages, including, but not limited to, special, incidental, consequential or other damages. The reader is responsible for their own choices, actions, and results.

The author can be reached as follows:

Email: Janice@divorcing-religion.com

Website: https://www.divorcing-religion.com

Podcast: https://www.divorcing-religion.com/religious-trauma-podcast

Published by Prominence Publishing. www.ProminencePublishing.com

Divorcing Religion/Janice Selbie. -- 1st ed.

ISBN: 978-1-990830-69-3

Praise for Divorcing Religion

"The first half of this book, Janice Selbie's memoir, tells a gripping tale of her journey from a constricting and repressive religious life to the freedom and joy of being self-responsibly nonreligious. She is remarkably candid about the challenges, both before and after leaving her faith. The story is of amazing courage and the book an engaging read. The second half provides valuable guidance for others in recovery from harmful religion, including exercises developed in her counseling practice."

—Marlene Winell, Ph.D.,
author of "Leaving the Fold" and founder of Journey Free

"The concept of divorcing religion is an extremely appropriate model for many people leaving any religion. As a psychologist and founder of Recovering from Religion, I have seen consistent patterns of emotion and behavior in those who are deconverting. These patterns are very similar to the emotional and behavioral responses of people experiencing marital divorce. Janice Selbie has brilliantly captured the essence of the grieving, recovery and reconstruction process. This workbook is well designed to gently guide you through the emotionally difficult process of religious recovery. We will be recommending Divorcing Religion to our clients at Recovering from Religion."

—Dr. Darrel Ray, author of "Sex & God" and "The God Virus,"
founder of Recovering from Religion and The Secular Therapy Project

Dedication

To the cherished family and friends who loved me through it all: Thank you.

To My Favorite Scientist, Paul Hamel, for expanding my world and filling it with love. Thank you for your encouragement and support.

Jasmine and Mariah, I love you. Thank you for being so gracious and supportive along the way.

Cory, Heather M, Niki B, and Bonnie W: Your decades of friendship and support mean the world to me.

Special Thanks

To author Darcie Friesen Hossack for helping me refine the original Divorcing Religion Workshop. To Paul H, Erin D, and Mairi D, for reading through my first draft with such care.

I am grateful to Dr. Marlene Winell (Journey Free), Dr. Darrel Ray (Recovering from Religion), Courtney Heard (Porthos Marketing), and Heather Sharpe (Sherpa Group Events) for supporting my vision to bring the Conference on Religious Trauma to reality.

To my conference speakers and podcast guests: Thank you for sharing your courage and resources with those who need it most.

To fundamentalists everywhere who shrink their social circles in the name of holiness:

OUTWITTED

"He drew a circle that shut me out—

Heretic, rebel, a thing to flout.

But Love and I had the wit to win:

We drew a circle that took him in!"

(Edwin Markham, 1852-1940)

Table of Contents

SECTION ONE: MEMOIR 1

   INTRODUCTION 3

   CHAPTER ONE: GROWING UP FUNDY 7

   CHAPTER TWO: ADOLESCENT IDENTITY CRISIS 21

   CHAPTER THREE: THE CULT OF PURITY CULTURE 37

   CHAPTER FOUR: BLESSED UNION? 47

   CHAPTER FIVE: FUN(dy)TIMES AT BIBLE COLLEGE 61

   CHAPTER SIX: THE PASTOR DISASTER 77

   CHAPTER SEVEN: MY EXTIMONY: WHY I LEFT CHRISTIANITY ... 91

   CHAPTER EIGHT: GOODBYE, PURITY CULTURE! 109

   CHAPTER NINE: ALL THAT GLITTERS 125

   CHAPTER TEN: READY, SET, GROW! 139

   CHAPTER ELEVEN: CLIENT STORIES............................ 161

SECTION TWO: WORKBOOK...179

   WELCOME 181

   MODULE ONE: BREAKING UP IS HARD TO DO:
      Realizing it's over..185

MODULE TWO: (Un)COMFORTABLY NUMB:
  Grieving Your Losses 195

MODULE THREE: THE SEPARATION AGREEMENT:
  Healthy Boundaries 217

MODULE FOUR: Getting Along with Yourself and Your Ex 231

  Part A: IDENTITY RECONSTRUCTION 231

  Part B: PURITY CULTURE RECOVERY 238

  Part C: LIFE PHILOSOPHY 252

MODULE FIVE: INTEGRATING YOUR LOSSES:
  Reframing and Rituals 267

MODULE SIX: PLENTY OF FISH:
  Finding and Building Your New Communities 277

MODULE SEVEN: MIND CONTROL:
  Don't Let an Old Flame Burn You Twice 291

FINAL THOUGHTS 309

ABOUT THE AUTHOR 311

SECTION ONE: MEMOIR

INTRODUCTION

On December 26, 2004, an earthquake in the Indian Ocean caused the deadliest tsunami in history, killing more than 230,000 people. With no warning, villages and families were wiped off the face of the earth. In an instant, loved ones became nothing more than a memory. Confused, wounded, and heartbroken survivors were left to piece their lives back together in the wake of unprecedented tragedy.

But where do survivors turn for comfort when the ones who provided comfort are no longer there? To whom does one pour out their heart when robbed of spouse, children, parents, and friends? In the face of unbearable loss, the world no longer makes sense. Formerly firm concepts like justice, security, order, and Divinity disintegrate in the face of such epic calamity. Sanity, itself, can come into question when mourning multiple significant losses in a short period.

While that devastating natural disaster happened in 2004, today I work with those who have suffered the emotional and psychological tsunami that accompanies the loss of religious faith and worldview. Once stable and secure, my clients are plunged into chaos with the dissolution of their core beliefs, the loss of their support system, and a massive breach of identity upon discovering that they were falsely indoctrinated. Their previously predictable lives become unrecognizable as formerly revered rituals, caring communities, and trusted touchpoints dissolve around them.

INTRODUCTION

My name is Janice Selbie. I am a professional counsellor and coach working with people recovering from Religious Trauma Syndrome. In addition to losing their core beliefs about the universe and God, many of my clients have been shunned by their families and religious communities upon losing or leaving their faith. Some are literally forced out of their homes and onto the street without adequate education, financial support, or even a basic knowledge of computers, banking, or how to drive a car. They are completely alone.

Growing up in a fundamentalist religious home can be an isolating and insulating experience when contact with the outside world is discouraged or forbidden. This can result in a lack of access to education - and even to basic healthcare.

Some clients come to me lacking a birth certificate or primary school education, having been poorly homeschooled by fanatical religious and anti-government parents; others reach out to me holding now-worthless doctoral degrees from religious institutions, no longer able to earn a living by preaching or teaching what they now know to be false.

For survivors of religious trauma syndrome, learning that they've been falsely indoctrinated is a jarring, disorientating, and grief-inducing trauma. Sadly, I, too, have experienced that trauma.

WHAT IS RELIGIOUS TRAUMA SYNDROME (RTS)?

According to American psychologist and author, Dr. Marlene Winell:

Religious Trauma Syndrome is the condition experienced by people who are struggling with leaving an authoritarian, dogmatic religion and coping with the damage of indoctrination. They may be going through the shattering of a personally meaningful faith and/or breaking away from a controlling community and lifestyle. RTS is a function of both the chronic abuses of harmful religion and the impact of severing one's connection with one's faith. It can be compared to a combination of PTSD *and* Complex PTSD (C-PTSD).[1][2]

RTS often results from being raised in a shame-based, emotionally dishonest, emotionally dangerous childhood environment where we were threatened with not only eternal damnation but parental alienation for the "sin" of disbelief. Societies around the world must recognize that religion is not always benign. For many, religion is harmful — and for some, it proves deadly.

While my own former religion (evangelical Christianity) taught me that I must love all people, it also taught me that those who did not adhere to my beliefs were dangerous and that I had to control my children to keep them from that danger. Unfortunately, this was only the tip of the twisted belief iceberg that made up my faith.

After nearly 4 decades as a devout Christian, reality came crashing down and shattered my faith. I now work as a Registered Professional Counsellor and religious trauma recovery coach, helping clients around the world come to terms with the monumental losses that accompany losing and leaving their religious faith. In addition to working individually with clients, I run support groups; facilitate the Divorcing Religion Workshop; founded the Conference on Religious Trauma and the Shameless Sexuality: Life After Purity Culture conference; and host the Divorcing Religion Podcast. I am also currently working with American colleagues to open the first religious trauma recovery center in the USA.

What follows is my personal *extimony* (the reversal of my former religious testimony) from Christianity, along with a Survival Handbook for those who, like me, end up Divorcing Religion and embracing reality.

---

[1] https://www.journeyfree.org/rts/
[2] https://en.wikipedia.org/wiki/Religious_trauma_syndrome

INTRODUCTION

The Survival Handbook is based on the Divorcing Religion Workshop © which I continue to offer online and in person.

The stories that follow are my own, true to the best of my recollection. Names have been changed, except where permission was granted.

Links to resources mentioned in each chapter and module can be found on the Divorcing Religion website https://www.divorcing-religion.com/ using the QR code (below) found at the end of each chapter and module. Resources on the website are listed in the same order in which they were mentioned.

LINKS & RESOURCES

CHAPTER ONE

GROWING UP FUNDY

My mother's parents were nominal protestant Christians who did not attend services regularly. My father's parents were "Christian Scientists," who believed that disease and illness were not real because the human body and material world were mere illusions (see Chapter 1 Resources). This inaccurate teaching, coupled with my grandparents' resultant refusal to believe he was sick even when he had a fever, likely contributed to my father becoming a raging hypochondriac by the time I was born.

Me with my brothers

While my parents were not religious when they married, my mother did comment that my father was much easier to live with after he "got saved." Had anyone asked me or my siblings, though, *easy* is not a word we would have ascribed to him.

HOLY ROLLIN'

The 1970s were a time of radical change in North America, including in the Christian church. As a child, I loved the sacred music of our services and felt swept up in the solemn beauty of hymns that reinforced our Christian tradition.

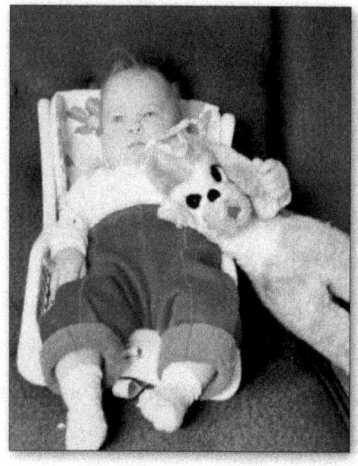
Welcome to 1970

One of my happiest church memories is of my parents standing me on the pew in between them, letting me hold the hymnal before I could even read the words. Sunlight streamed down on us through the colored glass windows, and I felt loved and doted on by my parents. Group singing evokes strong emotions in me to this very day. I now recognize it as a tactic to induce group bonding—plus a great way to facilitate memorization of Bible verses.

Soon, though, barefoot hippies and long-haired Jesus People made their way to our little Apostolic Church of Pentecost, bringing with them a new style of worship music. The lyrics were broadcast on a screen at the front of the church by an overhead projector since they were not in our beloved hymnals.

Featuring lots of repetition, the new songs, referred to as *choruses*, were catchy, emotional, and easy to learn. Some were slow and deeply moving, leading parishioners to raise their hands toward heaven and close their eyes, tears streaming down their faces as they sang.

Getting approval for drums to be permitted in services took some convincing, but once they were allowed our worship time would never be the same. Lively and upbeat, the days of somber organ music became a thing of the past. Along with drums and guitar, some of the ladies in the congregation would shake tambourines, and now loud shouts of "HALLELUJAH!" punctuated both the songs and the sermons in our sunny little cinderblock church.

To me, these are the very best memories of church and religion: Corporate worship of a loving God we could call upon, day or night, to ease our burdens and heal our wounds. Ours was a community of (mostly white, outwardly heterosexual) like-minded folks who cared for one another when times were hard.

I struggled with my hearing in childhood and still remember my parents and other congregants anointing my forehead with oil and earnestly entreating God for my total hearing restoration. I had complete trust in my parents and other adults from our church, as well as in God Himself.

My father was a strong, blustery, charismatic man who often served on the church board. I still remember him standing tall in the church doorway in his powder blue polyester leisure suit. With his Bible in one hand, his other hand would clap male parishioners on the back, as he enthusiastically greeted church members: "Good morning, brother! Hello, sister! God is great, amen?"

The charming, affable fellow who was admired by churchgoers had likely been yelling at his children to "Clam up!" in the station wagon as he stomped on the gas to ensure us first place in the church parking lot. Sunday mornings were stressful as we rushed to get dressed in our best clothes, eat breakfast without spilling on them, and brush our unruly hair into submission. For my mother, sister, and I, this also meant searching frantically for clear nail polish to curb runs in our pantyhose or leotards. With all that done, my father played race car driver to get us to God's House on time.

My mother, as gentle and kind as her husband was loud and brash, felt strongly that all newcomers must be welcomed into our home, as well as the church. Consequently, after Sunday service, our station wagon would be jammed with singles who had visited our church and were now joining us for a time of fellowship around our kitchen table.

Mom was careful to do her grocery shopping on Saturday, not wanting her dollars to support businesses that were open on the Lord's Day. I would go with her to the deli as she picked up buns, cold cuts, cheese, and salad fixings to be enjoyed at our lively Sunday luncheons. I felt happy to be included in such joyful, grown-up occasions.

Our 1970s Christian family (author seated next to mother)

WHERE SISTERS COME FROM

My parents were approved by the government to be foster parents, and my mother was especially interested in providing me with a sister. One morning when I was four years old, Mom happily informed me that it was a special day because it was the day I was getting a big sister. I had no better idea about where sisters might come from, and the thought of having another girl around to play with seemed like fun.

Sure enough, the doorbell rang a little later. I watched as Mom opened the door to a smartly dressed Caucasian woman in a tan pantsuit and a little Indigenous girl clutching a blue suitcase.[3] I figured this must just be how sisters come into the world.

The little girl was introduced to me as Sandra. She had darker skin than mine and shiny black hair, and when she smiled, she had a front tooth missing that she proudly told me had fallen out so a new one could grow in its place.

Sandra seemed physically fragile compared to our sturdy family of Scottish heritage, and I was surprised to learn that she was seven years old, as she wasn't much taller than me. After introductions were made, I asked my new sister if she wanted to play, and off we went.

GOD SPEAKS... SORT OF

One day, my parents packed up me and my three siblings and we headed off in our station wagon to Lima, New York, with our tent trailer wobbling behind us. My father was certain he had heard Jesus *personally* calling him to attend Elim Bible Institute there. Mom wasn't so sure when Dad first stated that he ALONE was called to move to the USA. Wisely, she informed him that God either called all of us or none of us – so off we went on our holy adventure from British Columbia to New York.

For the next year, each school day began by reciting the Pledge of Allegiance to the United States at Lima Christian School. For me, it was grade one, the year that I learned to read. This brought my teachers no end of amusement upon our return to Canada, where they had me read out loud in my New York accent.

---

[3] For more about Canada's historical mistreatment of Indigenous peoples, I recommend the book *Stolen from Our Embrace*, by Suzanne Fournier and Ernie Crey, Douglas & McIntyre (2013).

I don't recall very much about that year in NY, other than I lived in fear of earning a "demerit" at our school for doing something wrong. Three demerits meant a trip to the principal's office and getting whacked with a large wooden paddle on your rear end. Demerits were given out for infractions like talking in class, being up without permission, or failing to do homework. I suspect that this early threatening experience contributed to my dangerous obsession with rule-following.

Entrance to Elim Bible Institute, Lima, NY, 1975

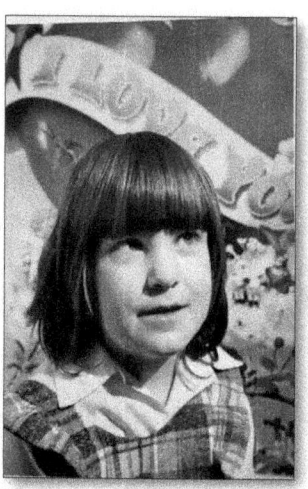

Grade 1

After a year of attending Bible College classes, my father felt he had learned enough to be a pastor, even though most pastors in mainline denominations are required to attain a 4-year degree. He declared our American adventure was finished, and we made the long drive back. My siblings and I were happy to be moving back to our old home and public school in Canada, where no one was allowed to paddle anyone else. We soon settled back into our usual rhythm.

Our year in New York coincided with the American Bicentennial, with fire hydrants painted like famous presidents.
I am the child leaning on George Washington.

Unfortunately for my father, but fortunately for the congregation of their long-time church, the elders, deacons, and pastoral team did not feel that Dad was suited for pastoral ministry and heading up a church after a single year of schooling. This was a shock to him, leaving him disappointed and angry over their decision. When a self-absorbed, vain person does not get their way, they become a force to be reckoned with. When said person happens to be male and a religious fundamentalist, not getting their way can be a breeding ground for abuse "in the name of Jesus."

WHEN GOD IS A NARCISSIST

It seems to be true that either narcissistic males are drawn to fundamentalist religions, where they can exercise authority without question, or fundamentalist religions breed narcissism in boys and men. According to the Bible, women are not fit to lead or have authority over men; they are not even to *speak* in church. This gives adult men, and sometimes even adolescent boys, total power over women and children in their religious communities and homes.

As with many religious families, money was always tight for us. My father abandoned higher education in his early 20s, though he had received a scholarship. His narcissistic personality made it hard for him to cope with opinions different from his own, and he was quick to take things personally. A phrase often heard in our home was "It's my way or the highway!" and he meant it.

As my earthly father, my dad was the closest representation of God available to me: Capricious, moody, powerful, and terrifying. His rejection by church leadership led to lots of yelling by Dad and lots of silent rage and crying by the rest of us.

While I couldn't name my feeling of powerlessness as a child, I remember my cheeks flaming, a lump forming in my throat, and balling my little hands into fists every time my father attempted to cut down my mother with his words. Instead of appreciating her, he regularly disparaged her in front of us. She was not his only victim, however. Even today, I vividly recall my huge father bounding up the stairs after me, shouting, "Stop crying or I'll give you something to cry about!" when I was just 8 or 9 years old.

No question existed in my mind that obedience was my best and safest option. I obeyed God, Jesus, my parents, my older siblings, Sunday school teachers, and anyone else in a position of authority. Sadly, I even obeyed older neighborhood kids and strangers, to my detriment.

Boundaries felt elusive to me. I had no concept of where others ended, and I began, which was a warning sign of the codependent traits I was witnessing and developing. I only knew that my role was to love everyone, accept everyone, and model Jesus at all times by being kind, forgiving, merciful, and compassionate. Nerds, outcasts, and manipulators gravitated to me because I was not permitted to set personal boundaries.

I had a love/hate relationship with my birthday because I could not just invite the girls I liked; I had to invite *all* the girls in the class, even the ones that picked their noses or didn't bathe regularly. In a fundamentalist Christian home, one quickly learns that sacrifice is expected in the short term, though not to be rewarded until the long term: Heaven.

GOOD GIRL

My siblings and I attended public school through grade 12, other than our one year of Christian schooling in New York. I remember my parents being upset when our public school board dropped daily Bible reading and recitation of the Lord's Prayer. If my parents knew that one of my teachers was a fellow Believer, they instructed me to invite the teacher to our home for dinner, which I faithfully did throughout elementary school.

Teachers loved me and requested to have me in their class, routinely noting on my report cards that I excelled academically and was mature, responsible, and diplomatic; a born leader (except for the fact that Christian females are not permitted to lead). As with many children who grow up in authoritarian religious homes, my carefree childhood was short-lived as I embraced the gravity of sin and Hell. I knew that my job was to always model Christ and set an obedient example for my classmates. For the same reason, bringing home anything less than top grades was not acceptable.

I cringe recalling the uncomfortable look on my school principal's face when he was delivering a science lesson to our grade 3 class about water. I took the opportunity to expound on the watery miracles found in the Bible: Noah's flood covering all creation, the floating axe head, and of course, the Lord Jesus himself walking on water. In my innocent and indoctrinated world, I assumed that our principal had just forgotten to include the miraculous in his lesson.

In grade 4, when our town's museum curator came to school to share some local history with us, I felt it my Christian duty to insist on being excused when he stated he would be opening his talk by reciting a traditional First Nation/Indigenous prayer in a local aboriginal dialect. Other students from Christian homes followed me out of the classroom, afraid they might offend God or be open to demonic influences by merely hearing a *heathen* prayer.

Grade 4 - Pentecostal Baptismal Candidate

I was formally baptized at Evangel Tabernacle Pentecostal Church at the age of 10. There was some debate as to whether I was mature enough to understand the significance of my decision, as the other congregants receiving baptism were adults. I assured them that I not only understood but felt it was the next required step in order for me to be a full-fledged witness for Jesus Christ.

That was good enough for Pastor Jack, who had me share my 10-year-old testimony from the baptismal tank before my holy dunking

Looking back, I wonder just what kind of dramatic conversion story they expected from a child whose only experience was that of being raised in a Christian home.

We attended Evangel church until a split over charismatic doctrine occurred, at which point my father felt led to take us in another direction, and we began attending a new church that formed out of that split: Sun Valley Interdenominational (but wholly charismatic) Community Church.

We bounced to several different charismatic churches throughout my childhood, staying until either my father felt offended (known in

Christian terms as being "righteously indignant") by a certain stance the pastor took or until God Himself told my father that we were to leave.

In my childhood experience, a church could splinter for many reasons, causing members to abandon their congregations – previously having been embraced as Church Family - and take up residence elsewhere. This felt confusing and unsafe to me as a child. Which church was the REAL church, where God's laws were adequately obeyed, and Jesus was exalted? Would members from the other church still get into Heaven? Would I still get to play with the kids whose parents stayed?

RAPTURE ANXIETY

In grade 5, my father informed me that I was not to participate in any lecture or event at school that focused on recycling or saving the environment, since those things were communist and "of the world." To evangelical Christians, the Earth is merely a temporary playground until we abandon it for heaven through either death or The Rapture.

The Rapture is an end-time Christian belief that when all prophecies are fulfilled then all true Believers, alive and dead, will be swept up to heaven. They believe literally that dead Christians will rise out of their graves and join the living who are sucked up into the clouds to meet the Lord. The exact date for the Rapture has never been figured out, though not for lack of trying over the centuries.

In the 1970s, and then again in the 1990s, movies were made about The Rapture to terrify nonbelievers and Christian children. My siblings and I watched these films at church and spent years terrified afterward. Anytime we came home to an empty house, a chill ran through us that we had not been good or holy enough, and our parents had been caught up in The Rapture while we were Left Behind (which is the actual title of one of the Christian novels exploiting this hot topic in 1995). There is even a name for those of us who suffered through these End-Time fears: *Rapture Anxiety*.

I remember discussing the Rapture with other children, trying to imagine the horror of those left behind when pilots and bus drivers would suddenly vanish into the clouds, leaving only their clothes behind in the driver's seat of a vehicle filled with terrified, doomed passengers. This part of the idea was titillating, considering all those naked people leaving Earth together in one giant SWOOSH! However, the Bible writers assured us that in heaven there is neither male nor female, so the naked part didn't count – though I did wonder how the holy neutering might occur.

Grade 5 was the year that we learned about our bodies in public school. To my horror, my mother felt the need to attend the "sex education" film and lecture we received at school after we were separated by gender. Apparently, she was worried the film might go too far in teaching us about our own bodies.

It's a good thing I saw it since that would be the only sex education I would receive. When I started menstruating at age 10, my father ominously warned me: "If you ever come home pregnant, don't bother coming home at all." Unfortunately, this just left me with a vague and threatening notion that getting my period was dangerous. After attending our one afternoon of sex education, I had many questions that I firmly understood I was to keep to myself.

Grade 7 was an important year, as it was our last year before moving to junior high school. To honor us in our final year of primary school, our principal hosted an annual event for grade 7 students that he called "The Great Greek Feast," since it was our year to learn about Greek mythology. There was much handwringing over whether or not my father would permit me to attend such a blatantly *non-Christian* event. Happily, he relented, and I attended as Alexander the Great — a detail I chose not to share with my father.

At the start of that same year, my parents contacted our principal to ask that I be enrolled in a different grade 7 class since they suspected the teacher was gay. I am grateful that the teacher phoned my parents to personally ask that I be permitted to remain in his class. When I think of how difficult that call must have been for him, my heart aches. I am delighted that my mother agreed for me to stay in his class, as it remains one of my best-loved school years. He was a fun and engaging teacher, and I am proud to say that I was his student.

Even though teachers thought I was great, I knew I would never be one of the cool or popular kids because I didn't swear and was an absolute goody two shoes. If I heard about an upcoming fight after school, I immediately reported it to a teacher. On the playground, if I noticed kids picking on another student, I would either insert myself into the dialogue by urging kindness or enlist the help of a teacher to stop the bullying. Far from respect, my efforts to protect and serve my classmates earned me an appropriate nickname: The Constable.

One incident stands out as a great example from when I was 11 or 12 years old. Wanting some independence, I bussed to the mall with a Sunday school friend who was a year or so older. She was a bit edgy, and both sets of parents hoped I would be a good influence on her. After trying on clothes and following boys around the mall (from a distance, of course), we were headed to our bus stop when she told me she had used her "5-finger discount." Since I had no idea what she meant, she pulled a bikini out of her purse to show me, having stolen it from the last store we visited.

Aghast, I insisted that she take it back immediately or I would leave her at the bus stop and never speak to her again. I was angry that she had stolen and angry that she told me about it, making me complicit in her thievery. She rolled her eyes and tossed the bikini on the floor just inside the mall door. After our bus ride home, I never heard from her again. FYI: In my 50s, I *still* find it hard to break rules – and I'm okay with that.

CHAPTER 1 LINKS & RESOURCES

CHAPTER TWO

ADOLESCENT IDENTITY CRISIS

My worldview, as one utterly indoctrinated by Christianity, was rigid and authoritarian. The notion of "live and let live" did not exist, in my home or my heart; there was only good or bad, with nothing in between. Any friends I had who were not Christians were viewed as *potential* Christians, and I was always on guard for opportunities to share my faith and spread the Gospel.

As I entered adolescence, however, body changes and raging hormones began to clash with the demand for puritanical thoughts and behaviors; I felt pulled in two directions. My early physical maturation made me look several years older than I was, and the attention I started receiving from older boys felt good. With an exhausted mother and a self-centered father, attention for me was in short supply.

My siblings all stopped attending church around the age of 12. I vividly recall feigning illness one Sunday morning to stay home with them, with my eldest brother playing a forbidden song on the family hi-fi: Raise A Little Hell, by Canadian rock band Trooper (*Thick As Thieves*, MCA, 1978). He did not play it quietly, either. My eyes grew wide and my pulse quickened with the heavy, driving beat. I loved the music but felt afraid of the feeling of rebellion rising in me.

My parents' deep sadness at my siblings' rejection of Christianity was obvious. I hated the thought of adding to that pain, but the freedom of sleeping in and staying home unsupervised on Sunday mornings was intoxicating. For a brief time, I chose the latter, feeling ready to take a walk on the wild side.

Yearning to be as cool as my big brother, I sought out edgier teens to hang around with. I even tried smoking, until my father found a cigarette in my jean jacket. The fact that he made this discovery while we were in a restaurant did not curb his angry tirade, and I recall slinking back to the car in humiliated silence. Though my rebellious phase lasted throughout my grade 7 year, I never did try smoking again.

Mom and Dad became especially concerned during the Grade 7 Rebellion when I began spending time with a new girl in our class who lived in foster care. Tough and pretty, "Crystal" was from a First Nations family and was largely avoided by our classmates. She smoked and swore and fought anyone who disrespected her. I told my folks I was trying to be a good influence on her, but they thought it unlikely and transferred me to a school in a different neighborhood for grade 8.

Grade 8 was a sad and lonely year without the kids I'd grown up with, even though my relationships with them were fraught. The only other familiar person in my new school was one of my brothers, but I wouldn't be interacting much with him there since he was in grade 11.

By the time I was 14, loneliness helped me to once again see the (religious) light. Determined to make my way back into the good graces of both God and my parents, I decided to return to the church of my baptism and attend services regularly. I did so on my own, as my parents continued church-hopping due to my father's righteously indignant tantrums.

LOVE BOMBING

That same year, an older girl of 19 took an interest in me at a church service and decided to make me her pet project. Being the youngest in my family and now a teen, attention at home was in short supply. By this point, my parents were tired after my first three siblings and took a more "hands-off" approach to parenting me. It seemed I could go days without seeing my siblings, who were now busy working and dating. I was often alone and yearning for an identity that fit.

For these reasons, I was utterly vulnerable to the love-bombing from the older girl (I'll call her Jane) and other church members. If you're not familiar, love bombing is exactly what it sounds like: One person pays so much positive attention to another that their target believes they are entering into a wonderful new relationship where they feel seen, heard, and valued. This tactic is used to woo new partners into romantic relationships, friendships, and religions/cults/high-demand groups.

To me, Jane was mature and thoughtful, pure and wise. I became utterly enamored of her and wanted to be like her in every way. She was very generous with her time, provided we spent it reading the Bible and other books that encouraged holiness and promoted obedience. I even remember sitting in my bedroom trying to emulate her handwriting. I kept every note she wrote me tacked to my bedroom wall, in the hopes of becoming a better Christian, just like her. To me, Jane epitomized the Virtuous Woman spoken of in the book of Proverbs. Plus, she was tall and slender, two things I would never be. Her natural good looks didn't even require makeup; everything about her was pure and perfect.

I, on the other hand, struggled with my weight, my temper, and my twin needs for attention and approval. I threw myself into Pentecostal charismatic Christianity with true zeal. Looking and acting much older than my early teens, I fit in easily at young adult services rather than in the youth group. I joined the young adult drama team and began performing with the praise and worship team, helping to lead the singing that I loved so much. Fellow worshippers in the group assumed I was the same age as they were, in my 20s. Surprise abounded when I invited a select few over for my 15th birthday party.

While I was accepted at church, I felt desperately alone at my new school and clung ever more tightly to my religious faith, attending services twice every Sunday as well as numerous nights each week. Being a "silent witness" was not enough; I was determined to be a true soldier of Christ, not some lukewarm wannabe!

Consumed with being a witness for my faith, I wore t-shirts emblazoned with Bible verses, carried a Bible at all times, advocated for a Christian Club, and shared the gospel by taping Bible verses and Christian song lyrics to the wall of the girls' bathroom.

Blinded by faith, I failed to see my own contribution to the vicious cycle that developed: The more snubbed and ostracized I was by my peers, the more obnoxiously judgmental and dogmatic I became, leading to the further annoyance and provocation of my classmates. As taught in evangelical circles, I knew that those who follow Jesus should expect persecution – a belief that fed my righteous misinterpretation of the bullying I received.

MARCHING FOR JESUS

In grade 9, my religious zeal had reached its zenith, making me the target of a group of kids who bullied me relentlessly. This, my first experience with being bullied, truly shocked me. At my old school, where we had all known each other since kindergarten, nobody was unkind to me. Since I was never unkind to others, I figured it just made sense that the world was filled with relatively decent people going about their business.

In this school, sometimes kids broke into my locker and left nasty notes; other times, they followed me around and tried to get me to react to their snarky comments with decidedly un-Christ-like behavior. They would follow me down the hallway yelling, "Repent!" or fake cry, "Jesus, I'm *SO SORRY!*"

I was not the only student antagonized by this band of bullies. I remember, during one Home Economics class, a couple of the worst bullies were harassing a girl whose father had died, telling her that it was her fault. I was dumbfounded by their cruelty and immediately told the teacher - who proceeded to shrug her shoulders and do nothing. Shocking even myself, I raised my voice to the teacher and told her that it was her job to protect vulnerable students, and if she didn't do something about it, then I would. She then told the bullies to back off and made the other victim my new class partner.

I eventually tired of picking spitballs out of my hair and checking down hallways to avoid the gang. I was weary of ignoring them in class, constantly hissing innuendos at me like "Hey Church Girl! What do you do AFTER church? I have an idea!" I tried responding with kindness, then ignoring them altogether.

Once my locker started being pried open and books went missing, I had had enough. I didn't know what was taking Jesus so long, but I was done waiting for him to change their hearts while they made my life miserable.

When I tearfully confided in an older church friend about what was going on, she declared that we needed to gather a group to hold a prayer march at my school to "break Satan's stronghold." One evening, she gathered other young adults to march around my school seven times, just like biblical Joshua did to bring down the walls of Jericho. Prayerfully, tearfully, and at times shouting out Bible verses, we commanded Satan and his legions to leave my school – and me – alone.

Unfortunately, our mini "March for Jesus" didn't yield any changes in the bullies' behavior. Finally, I told my mother what was happening at school. She insisted that my older brother, who was then in grade 12, have "a talk" with the ringleader of the bully brigade. I recall that talk involving him slamming his fist onto a locker beside the much shorter bully's head and encouraging him to lay off, which helped some.

Eventually, a meeting was held in the vice principal's office between me and the head bully (who, ironically, bore the surname of Lord). Each of us had to explain to the VP what was going on. The bully was made to apologize and warned to stop picking on me and other students, and my life started to improve.

SATANIC PANIC

I could hardly be blamed for seeing the Devil everywhere, since the 1980s was the decade of the Satanic Panic. This era largely kicked off when a few Christian performers claimed to be ex-satanists, keeping gullible charismatic Christian audiences on the edge of their seats over stories about human sacrifice and other tall tales - all the while raising money to continue their "rescue" efforts. These "testimonies," some of which were featured in full-length books, were later exposed as fraudulent.

Further contributing to the Satanic Panic, accusing secular rock bands of "demonic backmasking" was all the rage at that same time. Supposedly, when certain songs were played backward, one could hear satanic messages that, when played forward, bypassed listeners' consciousness and implanted dangerous messages directly into the *un*conscious mind.

Christians loved to hate the songs Stairway to Heaven (Led Zeppelin, *Led Zeppelin IV*, 1971 Atlantic Records) and Hotel California (The Eagles, *Hotel*

California, 1977 Asylum Records) especially, for their evil backmasking and supposed references to Church of Satan founder Anton LaVey.

Never ones to pass on potential showmanship, Pentecostal circles popularized vinyl record-breaking and cassette-burning nights throughout the 1980s. At these special Youth Group events, Christian youth were encouraged to renounce secular music and toss their favorite tapes and LPs into bonfires, where they would burn in a blaze of glory for Jesus!

Not to be outdone, American evangelist Bob Larson, "the world's foremost deliverance minister and exorcist" (according to his website) launched his two-hour weekly call-in show Talk Back in 1982. Brother Bob made a Holy Ghost-filled spectacle on his show for teens, railing against rock music, rap, and role-playing games.

Eventually, Bob's main topics turned to satanism and "satanic ritual abuse," and he started performing on-air exorcisms of his callers. For a fee, though, Brother Bob would perform personal exorcisms over Skype (see Chapter 2 Resources).

HOLY ROLLING: THE MUSICAL VERSION

Though it felt like I was drowning in angst, there were some bright spots. Like other teens in the 1980s, I loved skating at our local roller rink. Flashing lights, a huge disco ball, and driving beats made for a high-energy night out. Those not skating on the rink stood around the perimeter and held out a hand to receive high-fives from the skaters, a small act that made me feel accepted in a big way.

Once I learned there was a *Christian* skate time, I was truly hooked. I went roller skating twice every week: Once to satiate my carnal music desires, and the other so I could rock out to my favorite contemporary Christian music bands like Stryper, DeGarmo & Key, and Petra.

My father only allowed certain secular music in our home when I was growing up, mostly ABBA. Favorite secular bands I listened to on my Walkman included Journey, Van Halen, and the Eagles. One artist who made me deeply uncomfortable, though, was Madonna. Whenever the song *Like A Virgin* came over the speakers, I skated off the rink and grabbed a Diet Coke. Her frank sexuality made me feel guilty just by listening.

With no words of concern from other adults or "unsaved" friends in my life, I continued deeper down the evangelical rabbit hole, seeking experiences that confirmed my beliefs about God and opportunities to share His love with others. My identity and ideology/beliefs were becoming intricately enmeshed. Instead of trying out new makeup and hairstyles like other girls my age, I spent hours each week in prayer and Bible reading. I prayed for my friends, teachers, pastors, missionaries, unsaved relatives (my siblings first and foremost), world leaders, celebrities, and strangers.

SPIRITUAL GIFTS

In addition to Sunday services, the young adult group, and the Christian Skate nights, I attended special intercessory prayer nights, hoping that I, too, would receive the "baptism of the Holy Spirit" and be able to speak in tongues.

Speaking in tongues, or *glossolalia*, is a big deal in Pentecostal circles. Tongues are said to be angelic languages, so it is thought to make prayers extra powerful. Since I grew up hearing my parents and other church members speak in tongues, it never seemed odd to me, just part of the Christian experience. It did seem like a performance when my father was the one doing it, but it didn't seem that way for everyone endowed with The Gift.

Speaking in tongues meant that the Holy Spirit was in attendance - *right in our midst!* - so it was an extra special time to be in church. It was considered a serious and powerful gift, not to be taken lightly.

A typical Sunday service at my Pentecostal church usually included a special time for speaking in Tongues. A reverent hush would fall over the congregation when the Pastor urged all who had the gift of Tongues to start speaking to God in their own prayer language, waiting to see if we received an interpretation of the Tongues.

Age 14 - Trying hard to be a good church girl

A holy murmur arose from every corner of the room as parishioners fervently sought God in their secret prayer languages, sometimes kneeling, elbows on the padded pews, hands clasped in prayer.

While the worship team continued to play, the two groups – singers and pray-ers – competed for God's attention. The murmur of unintelligible prayers rose in volume, competing with the music. Finally, the room erupted in a holy crescendo that sounded, to the uninitiated (who were not filled with the power of the Holy Ghost), much like a cacophony. Tongues were shouted over the top of the worship team, who were singing at maximum volume. After cymbals crashed violently, the pastor would dramatically shout: "STOP! Now, we wait."

You could have heard a pin drop as we reverently waited for someone to come forward with the interpretation of another person's heavenly prayer language, which could be an individual message or one for the whole church.

One time someone started yelling out their *Word From The Lord* before the pastor gave them his permission to do so. Pastor held up his hand and commanded: "Prophet, hold your peace!" and the uninvited word-giver clammed right up and didn't utter another unholy peep.

BUT WAIT... THERE'S MORE!

In addition to the gifts of tongues and interpretation, the Holy Spirit could give others, too. One gift that seemed especially glamorous to me was the gift of Prophecy. Prophecy was proof of a direct connection to God, who would provide the Prophet or Prophetess with otherwise unknown information.

Sometimes I tested myself to see if I had the gift of Prophecy by trying to guess what would happen next in a TV show or what a friend was going to say. However, Prophetic Words were not to be confused with the bedeviled psychics or charlatans offering their *counterfeit* gifts on afternoon talk shows. Psychics merely pretended to know the future or connect with the dead to make money – unlike true Men and Women of God.

Once, while swimming at an almost-saved friend's house, I lost a contact lens in her pool. Praying hard (for Lo, my lenses were new and very expensive), I felt certain that God was telling me to swim down to the bottom of the pool 7 times – just like the Israelites had marched around the walls of Jericho and my young adult supporters marched around my school 7 times – so that my faith itself would cause the missing lens to reappear.

I was embarrassed and disappointed when my not-quite-saved friend saw that the God of the Universe was either not able or not interested in resurrecting my contact lens. Plus, now I had water in my ears on top of not being able to see out of one eye.

Though I earnestly petitioned God for the gift of prophecy, it was not forthcoming. Tongues seemed a better bet, especially since the Bible declared it to be evidence of the indwelling of the Holy Ghost. I knew Jesus was in my heart, and if he was there then the Holy Ghost was there too – I just had to learn to reverently spit him out.

I *really* wanted to be able to speak in tongues. Then one night at a prayer meeting I received this most coveted gift: I, Janice, could speak in tongues. The sounds came tentatively at first, surprisingly reminiscent of my father's prayer language. Tears streamed down my cheeks as I laughed, whispered, and then shouted out my new heavenly vocabulary. Other attendees (now witnesses to my gift) were equally moved. I entered that meeting as a mere Christian, but I left as one endowed with the True Gift of the Holy Spirit. I was excited, after my older friend drove me home, to share the exciting news with my father. He proudly told my big brother, who just shrugged.

I made a mental note to pray for my brother in my new heavenly language. Since my prayers would be more powerful now, I felt certain it was only a short matter of time before all my siblings returned to the fold. Now that I could speak in tongues, I was truly filled with Holy Zeal. A few weeks later, my eldest brother brought a friend over. Seeing me writing furiously at the kitchen table, he asked what I was working on – and looked embarrassed when I told him I was writing a sermon against lasciviousness and licentiousness. I was 15 years old.

As spiritually exciting as my grade 9 year was, grade 10 was soon to be upon me – and I had no desire to stay in the hostile environment of my current school. Feeling Divinely inspired, I picked up a form from the junior high closest to my house (where all my elementary school friends attended). That night, fearing my mother might not support my desire to change schools, I prayerfully forged her signature to do so. Even though junior high only went from grades 8 to 10, I was determined to enjoy that final year with my old friends before moving on to senior high.

Apparently, God had also bestowed upon me the gift of Holy Forgery because I was welcome to attend my neighborhood school after submitting the aforementioned form. It felt good (or at least less threatening) to be back amongst familiar faces. I toned down my witnessing by dressing more like my peers and even allowed myself the pleasure of participating in our school musical: *The Sound of Music*. To no one's surprise, I was a shoo-in for the role of the head nun, the Mother Abbess.

Typecast in the school play

Grade 10

TRYING TO FIT IN

Finally, I was able to relax a little and allow myself to just enjoy being a teen – almost. I continued to attend church several nights per week. Still not able to keep my beliefs to myself, when our science teacher told us we had to make class presentations, I knew just what mine had to be about: ABORTION. I collected as many graphic – and sadly inaccurate - Christian pamphlets as I could from Keith Green's "Last Days Ministries" cult about the evils of abortion and got to work on my full-color display featuring photos of aborted fetuses.

When I finally gave my uncomfortably detailed presentation, the class sat in stunned silence. Even our teacher, a former police officer, looked shocked. I was so wrapped up in my personal belief system that it never crossed my mind that any of my classmates might have had abortions.

In fact, I was so disconnected from teenage reality that I would not even have believed any of them were having sex. *See chapter 2 Resources for the link to a podcast interview about the LDM cult.*

PARTY ANIMAL?

Safe to say that, after my wildly unpopular anti-abortion project, I didn't get invited to many parties in grade 10. To be precise, I was invited to only one, but it was a doozy. As one of the oldest in our class, I had my driver's license before most of the other kids. Still a goody-goody at heart, I knew I would not be drinking at the party so offered to be a designated driver for a group of girls I had known since early primary school.

My dad agreed to let me use his pickup truck on the evening of the party, though I didn't tell him where I was headed. Armed with my six-pack of Orange Crush, I picked up the other girls, who had managed to get their hands on assorted bottles and cans of alcohol. Excited, we drove to the outskirts of town where our classmate, affectionately dubbed Farmer Dave, was hosting the party on his family's huge property.

Boomboxes were blasting out popular 80s songs by Van Halen, Cindy Lauper, Judas Priest, and Madonna. The party was in full swing with kids getting plastered, throwing up, or pairing off. A huge bonfire was blazing, around which kids danced, played air guitar, and consumed copious quantities of "coolers," which were basically like soda pop with alcohol. I smiled and sang along with the music, feeling both excited to be attending such a raucous event and also like a huge fraud. Feeling conflicted was my new normal, and I worked hard to prevent the Holy Spirit from ruining my one "normal" teenage event.

Eventually, one of the girls told me our other friend wasn't doing very well. We found her throwing up behind a bale of hay and told her it was time to go home. My friends tossed their unopened six-packs into the back of the truck and then joined me in the cab. Ever concerned about safety and rules, I wouldn't start the truck until everyone had seatbelts on. We strapped the drunkest girl into the seat next to the passenger door, with the window open in case she was sick.

Careful to obey the speed limit, especially now that it was dark, I headed down the long, windy road into town. Unfortunately for me, my dad's truck was so old that the high beams were operated by a switch on the floor rather than accessible on the steering column. I didn't know my high beams were stuck until a police car drove past and pulled a U-turn, pulling up behind me with lights flashing.

As a new driver and an extreme rule-follower, my life flashed before my eyes as I slowly pulled over. I was extremely nervous and extremely innocent. When the officer shined his light in our cab and asked if I'd been drinking, I replied honestly "No, sir! I've only been drinking Orange Crush. See?" and then proceeded to stick out my tongue to prove my honesty.

Unsurprisingly, I was asked to step out of the vehicle. While I was performing such amazing feats as walking in a straight line and reciting the alphabet backward from Z, another officer was removing the six-packs from the truck bed and was mildly concerned about the severely intoxicated girl with her head hanging out the passenger window.

Convinced I was sober, the officers sent us on our way with strict orders to go straight home. As I pulled up in front of my drunk friend's house, she gave one last poorly aimed technicolor hurl, unfortunately spraying the inside of my dad's truck with her leftovers. I sighed and recalled the Bible verse that said: "And be sure, your sins will find you out."[4]

By the time I dropped off the last girl, I was too tired to deal with cleaning out the truck and went to bed intending to wake up early to clean it up.

---

[4] Numbers 32:23

My teen body had other plans, however, and I slept in. When I finally went downstairs, my father said the strangest thing had happened: When he got up in the morning, my young friend was cleaning out his truck while her father sat in his car, listening to music. For once, Dad thought better than to ask questions and simply appreciated his free truck detail. Thus endeth my high school partying days.

CHAPTER 2 LINKS & RESOURCES

CHAPTER THREE

THE CULT OF PURITY CULTURE

The best thing about grade 10 was meeting a boy who thought I was cute. We ended up transferring to the same school for grade 11, and I began my first romantic relationship. We dated through grades 11 and 12, falling in love and learning about partnership – all without ever having sex. My purity had to be maintained at all costs. That first boyfriend was patient, I'll give him that.

By the time grade 12 hit, my church attendance had severely waned. Since my love interest had no God interest, I chose to remain with the fleshly one who could actually hold my hand. I felt certain Jesus understood.

Uh oh – Mistletoe!

That first year of college, though, patience was in short supply for both me and my boyfriend. We knew we loved each other and were attracted to each other. For over two years we pushed our self-control to the absolute limits until I finally decided we were ready to consummate our relationship.

In love at high school graduation

To my total dismay and devastation, my first love – the one to whom I had given my most cherished possession (my virginity, according to Evangelical teachings on sexual purity) – no longer wanted me. My mother's voice rang in my ears, warning me not to engage in premarital sex because "Why would a man buy the cow if he can get the milk for free?" Looking back, it was insulting to be likened to a cow; but at the time, I felt like the dumbest female in history.

With his rejection, my world crashed down around me. All of the church teachings I had heard about premarital sex clanged in my ears. I was now Worthless! Used! Yesterday's news! Dirty! Sullied! Broken! Trash. I felt too disgusted with myself to return to church. I couldn't possibly fit in with those pure souls like Jane. Fearing that no one would ever want to be with me since I was no longer a virgin, I felt compelled to prove to myself that I was still desirable. I became a barfly, desperate for validation from any source.

With my broken heart and nonexistent self-esteem, I began a string of sad and lonely one-night stands. From 19 to 23, I sang in rock bands (which was fun, I must admit), moved to the Big City, and drank my way through countless nights, all the while feeling deeply guilty and conflicted about the life I was living. While I loved being on stage singing popular secular (i.e., non-Christian) songs, I "knew in my heart" that it was displeasing to God.

This is clear evidence of religious indoctrination: No longer did I need parents or pastors shaming me; I was able to shame myself, thus perpetuating the endless cycle of sin and repentance that Christianity is built on. True to my religious training, I feared dying while in a state of sin and being cast into the pit of Hell for all eternity. I could not continue in my tortured state. Something had to give.

I loved singing in my first band but struggled with guilt over the heathen lyrics

BORN AGAIN, AGAIN

One Saturday, an old friend from my hometown, now living in the big city, invited me to spend the weekend with her. She knew I was struggling and suggested that in the morning we attend church together even though neither of us had gone in a few years. We chose an evangelical "nondenominational" church (that means they did not identify as strictly Pentecostal, Baptist, Lutheran, etc. but were Bible based and likely charismatic) and sat near the back.

As fate would have it, the speaker that day talked about the prodigal son, the biblical parable about a wayward young adult who rejects working the family farm in favor of cavorting in the city. Eventually, said cavorter runs out of money and finds himself in a particularly dirty and offensive position trying to survive. His wealthy father, filled with forgiveness, sends servants to retrieve his wayward son and throw a huge feast to welcome him back.

What could possibly have been a better story for my guilt-ridden ears to hear? I was moved to tears: *God, Himself, was calling me home!* When the communion tray was passed around, I had a choice to make. Only true believers who are "right with God" are supposed to partake of the Lord's supper (in this case, tiny crackers on a plate and mini plastic cups filled with grape juice). I could feel my friend's eyes staring at me, wondering what I was going to do.

In an instant, I begged God's forgiveness for my wayward actions, asking Him to cleanse my filthy heart and mind and accept me back into the fold (literally, a pen to hold sheep; metaphorically, the family of God). Feeling instantly lighter, I joyfully partook in communion while my friend passed the plate without participating.

Having re-dedicated myself to God, I was once again consumed by familiar religious zeal. I went back to the house I shared with heathen roommates and told them my life was changing. For me, there would be no more drinking, parties, or romantic liaisons. I went through my bedroom and threw out anything I thought might be offensive to the Holy Spirit, getting rid of books, cassette tapes, and questionable clothing. On a mission to cleanse my whole life, not even our kitchen was safe. Feeling moved, I brazenly directed my roommate to remove the fake penis from our kitchen bulletin board.

I truly felt like a burden had been lifted because I was no longer wracked with guilt over living a god-free, religion-free life. My parents were thrilled, my roomies, not so much. Within a couple of months, I moved out on my own so that I didn't risk being corrupted by my pre-saved friends. I found a large Pentecostal church and attended at every opportunity, quickly joining the worship team, and becoming well known in the young adult group — where I finally was old enough to be a member, at age 22.

One Sunday morning at church, we were instructed to turn and greet our neighbors with a holy handshake. When I shook hands with the tall, handsome African man behind me, it felt like a jolt of electricity went through me. He felt it too and asked me to stay after service to chat with him. His name was Alex, and he was a former Olympian from the nation of Ghana.

Goodbye heathen fun, Hello Bible study

It didn't take long to see that Alex was somewhat smitten with me, but I wasn't sure I felt the same about him. I enjoyed his company, but he spoke often of returning to Ghana and wanting a Christian bride with him to help evangelize his nation. He tried to kiss me once, but to me, it did not feel "honoring to God." He was apologetic and never tried again. While not entirely attracted to him, I respected his religious fervor.

Eventually, he spoke to me in a serious tone. *"Janice, I have had a word from God. You are to be my wife and move with me back to Ghana."* This was very confusing to me because somehow I had missed that holy memo. I felt torn, wanting to please the Lord and be obedient, but not overly keen on moving to Africa. I decided to take a trip back to visit my parents, though I didn't tell them why.

One evening during my visit home, my mother entertained two retired missionary ladies. I was very interested to hear about their time in ministry, particularly when I found out they had served most of their years in Africa. As I asked them questions about Ghana, one of them became suspicious and asked me if I had received an offer of marriage from a Ghanaian national. I felt my cheeks flush bright red as I nodded, and I shared with them my uncertainty about the situation. I am thankful to this day for their unified response, as they both recommended that I reject the offer. I felt incredibly relieved and had no problem agreeing with them.

Belief in the supernatural left me vulnerable to others who espoused the same beliefs, particularly if they declared that they had the gift of prophecy. It is relatively easy for religious people to manipulate other religious people, particularly men with women. Alex believed that he had heard from God – and my belief in that same God, as well as the biblical teaching that women are to submit to men, caused me to question whether I should marry him and move to Africa, despite my misgivings. Well-meaning people end up living on cult compounds and enduring or even perpetrating horrendous abuse when a charlatan or delusional person convinces them that it is somehow Divinely ordained. Who are they to argue with *God's anointed*?

HOMEWARD BOUND

I returned to the city only to pack up my things and move back home. I would live with my parents either until I graduated from college or found a godly man to be my husband – provided he wanted to stay in North America.

While not thrilled to be in such proximity to my father again, I was grateful for the chance to live rent-free while attending school. I quickly joined the campus Christian group and began writing for and editing their Christian newspaper. Earnestly believing that the Bible was 100% literal and infallible, I eagerly attended seminars about Young Earth Creationism.

I was delighted to add books from organizations such as Answers in Genesis to my collection, studying them so that I would be ready to give an answer for my eternal hope to any nonbelievers the Lord might put in my path.

I also resumed my place in the Pentecostal College and Career group (a.k.a. Young Adults Ministry) I'd been part of formerly, which was now called the Refiner's Fire. This name was based on Bible verses that refer to God refining his chosen people through fiery trials, as well as a metalsmith using fire to separate or refine the impurities from precious metal.

Belonging to the Refiner's Fire Young Adult Christian Fellowship meant that we were set apart by God, to be purified by Him and used for His purposes rather than for our own. It sounds cultish to me now, but back then it played right into my belief that only God could know what was best for me, and only God Himself could discern what was true. In fact, growing up in a Christian environment I learned from a young age that I could not trust my heart, meaning my feelings or instincts. To Christians, "The heart is deceitful above all things and desperately wicked" (Jeremiah 17:9).

This is why it was so important for me to hear from my mother's missionary friends after receiving the marriage proposal. To me, those missionaries had proven themselves to be women after God's own heart, even foregoing marriage for the sake of spreading the Gospel. I didn't think I could trust what my own heart was telling me, which was to run far and fast from my African pursuer, but I felt pretty sure I could trust what *their* hearts told them. This notion that one cannot be trusted to discern truth or decide what to do without direction keeps Christians in a perpetual state of childlike dependence on their leaders.

Our Christian club at the college was aghast when a student pub was permitted to open on campus. So, as is a usual custom for Christians, we set up our own Christianized version, determined to make it much more fun and engaging with no alcohol. We hired Christian musicians and comedians, and lots of young adults from every church in town attended. However, we never did have much success making converts on campus, regardless of how modestly I dressed and how chastely I behaved.

**Studying "The Word" between classes,
praying not to become an old maid at 22**

Shockingly to me, some of my Christian righteousness was misinterpreted as self-righteousness, to which my decidedly secular classmates responded with irritation. Once again, my zealous love for Jesus cost me friendships.

I recall one student loudly declaring in class that "Jesus is nothing more than a dead man on a tree," at which I burst into tears and left the room. My identity had become so fully fused with my beliefs that her comment caused me true distress. As with the similar scenario in my adolescence, I told myself that I was being persecuted for the sake of the Gospel. This time, I could turn to many other Christians on campus when the burden felt too great. As before, they celebrated my persecution and reminded me that my reward in heaven would be great.

THE DATING GAME

During that year at college, no less than four of my Christian buddies from the college campus got engaged to be married, their ages ranging from 18 to 21. At 22, I was one of the oldest to still be single. I felt that they were passing me by and was concerned that I would become a spinster. My pastor must have felt the same, as he soon invited me to a dinner party thrown by him and his wife in their home. The guests included me and three single men from the young adult group. While they all recognized me from singing on the worship team, I did not know them.

Though I felt immediately attracted to the extrovert in the group, it was the serious and cerebral fellow who would end up asking me out. How cerebral was he? His friends called him "Mr. Spock," in reference to the pointy-eared Vulcan character on Star Trek who thrived on logic and eschewed emotions. While it would have been more light-hearted spending time with the fun-loving man, the gentle and quiet one had two things – the most important things – going for him in my deeply indoctrinated 22-year-old mind:

1. He was very committed to the Christian faith, and
2. He was tall.

Standards, y'all.

With our pastor's blessing, we began dating. This time, sex was not an option. When I lamented my impure status to my pastor, he informed me that I was forgiven and could consider myself a *secondary virgin*, which was almost as good as being a real one. Christians tend to marry young and after short engagements, to avoid falling into the dreaded sin of sex before marriage. Several quote 1 Corinthians 7:9 on this topic, convincing themselves that "It is better to marry than to burn with passion." Our pastor was delighted to marry us within the year, and I gave no more thought to continuing my education. Wifedom and motherhood were my Christian duty, and I was happy to oblige.

CHAPTER 3 LINKS & RESOURCES

CHAPTER FOUR

BLESSED UNION?

**Singing thank you to Jesus
(for not letting me be an old maid at the age of 24)**

The wedding reception was an alcohol-free, dance-free zone, held in the basement of my childhood church, The Apostolic Church of Pentecost. Money that would have otherwise been used to pay for booze and a band went instead to helium-filled balloons attached to large candy-filled brandy snifters. Christians pride themselves on eschewing worldly (adult) ways in favor of maintaining a child-like innocence, which was in full view at our reception. The jokes and music, much of which were performed by the bride and groom, were God-rated.

At the end of the night, we left for a local hotel. Thankfully, our pastor warned us that many newlyweds find themselves too exhausted after the wedding festivities to consummate their marriage on the wedding night. This proved true for us, and we fell fast asleep in the same bed without doing more than holding hands. Our pastor's words relieved us of feeling pressure or shame about our lack of wedding night sex. However, I did hear my delightfully innocent husband repeating a Bible verse until he fell asleep beside me: "They were naked and not ashamed."

MARRIAGE TO MR. SPOCK

My studious and quiet husband often seemed oblivious to the feelings of others and frequently had a hard time understanding their distress over his brutally honest comments. To him, nothing was wrong with offering the whole truth in every instance. He lacked insight into social interactions, frequently offending others and not caring in the slightest. I recall attending a church gathering when he bluntly asked one of the ladies in attendance whether she dyed her hair. I nearly choked, seeing the mortified look on her face. I laughed nervously and interjected, "What next, dear? Are you going to ask her age? Ladies don't answer such questions," and then quickly moved him along to a different cluster of attendees.

Another time I waited in the car while he went into a small hardware store, followed by a somewhat plump young lady. When she exited a couple of minutes later in tears, followed by my husband looking sheepishly at the ground, I knew he was somehow involved. "Did you ask that girl if she was pregnant?" I demanded. "Yes, but I don't know why she was so upset! She said she isn't pregnant, so what's the big deal?" Unfortunately, these would not prove to be isolated incidents through the course of our marriage – making his social interactions taxing for me.

I recognized that "until death do us part" was going to be an extremely long time when our first Valentine's Day as a married couple came and went with no recognition on his part. When I realized he had not made any dinner reservations, I called multiple restaurants which were, of course, full. What was more troubling to me was that he had not even bothered with a card, let alone flowers.

This was the first of many extremely disappointing and emotionally painful holidays that simply meant nothing to him. Though I told him in no uncertain terms that those special days meant a great deal to me, they continued to fly under his radar. My tears did not move him; in fact, they seemed to steel him against me as he accused me of trying to manipulate him with my emotions. I had to accept the reality of life with a partner who felt more like a robot. I suspected he might have Asperger's syndrome, or neurodivergence, but I could do nothing about it.

HEAVENLY RECEPTION

Shortly after moving to Vancouver in our first year of marriage, a friend got me a job as a receptionist for a major payroll company. I was excited to have what felt like my first professional Big City job, where I had to dress up every day. I took my role seriously as the first person any client would encounter, either in the office or on the phone. My goal was to always display the love of Jesus.

I used thumbtacks to discreetly pin a couple of Bible verses in my cubicle, reminding me to keep a cheerful countenance:

- ✝ A happy heart makes a cheerful face.

- ✝ A cheerful look brings joy to the heart of another.

In the days before the internet, people calling a payroll firm were either only interested in quickly dictating numbers to their service agent... or angry that an error had been made on their account. I could usually win cranky clients over with my delightful demeanor, but one particular man was a force to be reckoned with each time he called.

Mr. Dyck (surprisingly, *not* his real name) operated several different companies in western Canada and used our payroll service for all of them. He never returned any greeting no matter how pleasantly I answered. Instead, he just growled or yelled the name of his service agent. If they were busy with another client or simply did not want to talk with the grumpy curmudgeon, I had to deal with him myself.

It became obvious that simple cheerfulness was not going to work with Mr. Dyck. My cubicle became FILLED with additional Bible verses to help me hold my temper during his calls:

- ☦ A gentle answer turns away wrath.

- ☦ A fool gives full vent to his spirit, but a wise man quietly holds it back.

- ☦ A hot-tempered man stirs up strife, but he who is slow to anger quiets contention!

- ☦ THE VEXATION OF A FOOL IS KNOWN AT ONCE, BUT THE PRUDENT IGNORES AN INSULT!!!!

It's safe to say that Mr. Dyck stretched my capacity for maintaining a pleasant and professional demeanor to its absolute limits. I even requested to attend a special class on customer service to try and help me figure out how to best serve this particularly demanding client. There, I was instructed to practice active listening and repeat to the client what I thought he was asking.

Finally feeling equipped for the task, I looked forward to Mr. Dyck's next call. When his cantankerous voice demanded to speak with his service agent, I sweetly informed him that she was on her break but would call him as soon as she returned. As his volume increased, I practiced my newfound active listening skills - to which he replied *"Did you just swallow a parrot?!* I want you to put my agent on the phone NOW!"

So much for HR supplying me with the holy grail for customer hotlines. I was at my wits' end with Mr. Dyck. I had fasted, prayed, memorized scriptures, and done everything else I could think of to end his abuse. I had reached my breaking point.

The next time he called, I patched him through to his agent as quickly as possible. When the call bounced back to me, he was already breathing heavily. I warned him that if he raised his voice or cussed at me, I would hang up. Unsurprisingly, he did. Very surprisingly, *I* did. As good as it felt to disconnect him mid-swear, I was also terrified. Though my heart frantically pounded in my chest, I knew I had to answer that phone when he called back, livid that I had hung up on him.

In my most cheerful tone, I answered with my usual full spiel. When he started yelling again, I transferred him - directly to the Vice President of Western Operations. With no warning. I tried to avoid eye contact with the VP as she stared daggers at me through her office window while trying to calm the raging Mr. Dyck. I prayed mightily for wisdom as she walked out of her office and over to my desk, my throat suddenly dry.

When the VP asked what had happened to make me transfer a service call to her, I tearfully explained that I had tried every way I knew of to serve Mr. Dyck as a faithful Christian, but none of them had worked. I had transferred his call to her because he was a bully with all the power, and she was the most powerful person I knew in that office.

Observing the now *massive* collection of Bible verses I had tacked up on my workstation like some sort of protective shield, the VP smiled kindly at me and told me she understood. From now on, I was to patch him through directly to her, and she would deal with his cranky ass. Jesus might have been too busy, but that VP had my back.

While I worked hard to control my temper and share the love of Jesus as a receptionist, my new husband worked equally hard fending off unwelcome male advances at his hair salon. His gentle demeanor while working as a hairstylist led to some uncomfortable interactions with clients who assumed he was gay.

At first, he tried taping our wedding photo up at his station and hoping clients would ask him about it. I knew he'd given up on waiting for Jesus to intervene when he told me about an aggressive client who ignored our photo and tried to touch my husband without his consent. The client received a shocking knock on the head from hubby's blow dryer, along with a mumbled: "So sorry, it slipped." Like being a Christian in high school, being a Christian in the workplace was challenging.

Since we had not lived together before getting married, we had a lot to learn about each other and about how to co-exist as adult partners. Communication, which I had always prided myself on, seemed particularly challenging with my husband. While he was intelligent and typically kind, he seemed unable to respond or connect to me on an emotional level. It was like we spoke different languages.

WHEN SWEET TURNS SOUR

For the most part, I got along well with my husband – not that I had any other choice as a Christian woman. The only big fight I remember that first year was when he insisted that we continue attending a Pentecostal church that I felt was too extreme, even for me. I was fine with Tongues and even holy dancing - but being *slain in the spirit* was just too theatrical for me. To be slain in the spirit is to receive a powerful touch (literally, a touch from the pastor on your body) from the Holy Spirit that knocks you to the ground, as in a faint. It just seemed too phony.

The church we were attending even kept blankets on the front pews to ensure the modesty of any sister wearing a dress who might *get slain*. As soon as she had her holy swoon, an usher would quickly drape the blanket over her pantyhose-clad legs so that the sight would not "cause a brother to stumble."

I did not wish to keep attending any church that, in my righteously indignant opinion, made a mockery of the Holy Spirit. Alas, my husband was ever hopeful that he might be invited to become a staff member, either working with young adults or as a music pastor. On our drive home after one particularly irksome Sunday morning service (we went twice on Sundays and numerous weeknights), we got into a heated debate over whether to continue attending. It wasn't a debate at all, since he reminded me that he was the decision-maker in our marriage, and he wanted to keep going.

I demanded that he pull over and let me out of the car, which he did, shrugging his shoulders and driving off. I desperately wanted him to turn around and come back for me, but that did not happen. Tearfully, I walked the rest of the way home in my uncomfortable church shoes, unsure why God had ordained our painful union in the first place.

Wishing my husband would behave differently without me telling him about it became a hallmark of our difficult relationship. I bore the emotional pain and frustration like a martyr, as I'd been trained to do in both my church and my family of origin. My mother's example as a Christian wife was to silently accept all emotional pain inflicted by my father, and I followed that conditioning. I had no idea that this was codependent behavior.

MEETING GOD'S CHOSEN FROZEN

During our second year of marriage, we took a trip to Scotland to visit my relatives and see the sights. It was my husband's first time on a plane and my first trip to the UK. My cousin, an older lady who attended the Church of Scotland, was delighted to set up an opportunity for us to perform some music in her local Presbyterian church. The traditional conservative congregation, however, was caught off guard by our rather Pentecostal flavor.

Unfazed by the somewhat frosty reception from God's Chosen Frozen (a nickname charismatics use to describe *non*charismatic Believers), we set out to visit a Pentecostal Canadian couple we knew who were attending seminary at the University of Aberdeen, doing our best to encourage them to remain spiritually zealous in their new, more restrained, environment.

My cousins did their best to entertain us, taking us to visit their local minister. To our shock, he offered us whiskey – as did all the homes we visited. To their shock, we turned them down each time, wanting nothing to do with the Devil's brew.

While I enjoyed visiting with my cousins, my husband found it too tiring trying to understand their accents. We stayed for two weeks, and every night he retired to bed immediately after dinner, preferring to read his Bible and pray rather than get to know my kin. This embarrassed me deeply, but they graciously told me it was likely just jet lag (the longest case in history, apparently). I appreciated their kindness and did my best to enjoy our vacation.

CHARISMANIA

After our return, we decided to move back to our hometown. It felt good to be back. We began attending a different church, this one in the Vineyard movement, and much more charismatic than our former Pentecostal church - minus the spiritual slayings. The music at our new church was spectacular, spawning successful contemporary Christian music careers for many of the worship leaders.

To go along with the music, other roles for worshippers included flag waving (not flags from countries, but flags denoting holiness and calling people to worship), holy dancing (requiring modest clothing that had to be roomy enough for twirling and leaping if the Spirit so led), and banner making (similar to the flags, only with much more detail and on a larger scale). The Vineyard movement is extremely attractive to creative types wanting to use their gifts in God-approved ways. As usual, my husband was hopeful that he would be asked to join the staff as a preacher. He was very cerebral and loved apologetics.

Instead of inviting him to teach, they asked us both to become members of the worship team. I have always loved music and have a strong voice and a good ear. My wayward years spent singing in rock bands made me comfortable on stage. My husband, however, was not a singer. He taught himself guitar, though for him it was never natural, and he struggled to keep the tempo. At times, the difference between our skill levels caused me distress, though it did not bother him.

Early in our marriage, I had a guitar of my own; but we sold it when we were short of rent. I believed I should not play guitar anymore so that he could shine in that area. Likewise, I loved to write, but so did he – and I sincerely believed (thanks to my mother's codependent Christian example) that no wife should outshine her husband. Instead, I would throw myself into homemaking and child-rearing, though not terribly excited by either.

Try as I might to thrust my husband into the spotlight, I could not keep from garnering the attention of fellow musicians in our church who invited me to sing background vocals on an upcoming album. I was pregnant at the time, so didn't feel I had as much energy as usual, but I still readily accepted because I thought it would be a good opportunity to help further the Gospel. My husband had also rented studio space at local recording studios for us to record our original gospel music around that time.

I felt conflicted and uncomfortable after a quick, private conversation with a producer who happened to be in the same studio as us that day. He pulled me aside and told me that I had tremendous potential – but that I would never make it if my husband insisted on being my guitar player. Sadness and anger washed over me as I contemplated the life I might have had were I not tied to this man; this Godly, robotic, brilliant, rhythmically challenged man. I bit my tongue – again – and swallowed my pain.

WELCOME TO THE 'HOOD: PARENTHOOD

Preparing for the birth of our first child, we attended parenting classes at our local college. Of course, the parenting books I was reading were by Christian authors who espoused both the merits of discipline for even the youngest children and the dangers of spoiling them by picking them up when they cried or holding them for too long.

Christian parents hold to one verse as a promise if they effectively discipline their children: "Train up a child in the way he should go, and when he is old he will not depart from it (Proverbs 22:6)." No thought is more terrifying to a Christian parent than the possibility of their child rejecting the Gospel and spending eternity in Hell, separated from both them and God.

Another verse is used especially to defend the practice of spanking children: "Spare the rod and spoil the child" (Proverbs 13:24). Sadly, this verse is responsible for much child abuse in Christian homes. Along these important lines of properly disciplining children, I believed that babies needed to be put on a strict schedule. I was never to bend to their desires; they must learn from the start that Mother was in charge.

To that end, I would never feed "on demand" but only every 3 hours, as my Christian parenting books instructed me. When I mentioned this in our Public Health pre-parenting class, however, I received a resounding rebuke from both the nurse leading the class and the other parents who felt that our stance was bordering on abuse. I was both horrified and mystified about why they could have an issue with the very sound Christian rationale behind our plan. Once again, I chalked it up to nonbelievers being blinded by Satan. I forgave them for their blindness and comforted myself knowing that *my way* was more pleasing to God.

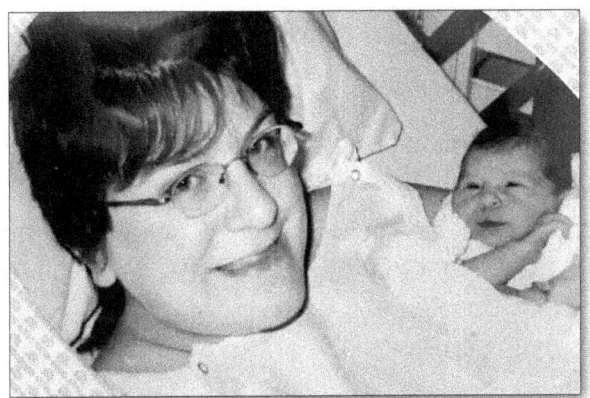

Praising Jesus – for an emergency C-section

Just a few days after our precious daughter was born, we were back in church and ready to "dedicate her to the Lord." We asked a couple we loved and trusted, who were themselves deeply indoctrinated by Christianity, to be her Godparents. They agreed and attended the service, willing to declare their support publicly. I was ecstatic to be a wife and mother helping to raise the next generation for God. What role could be more important than bearing children and raising them to serve Him? I was determined to do a better job than my own parents of ensuring my children did not stray from The Truth.

One thing I had looked forward to was attending Mom's Time Out at one of our local churches. I had started going with a friend when I was pregnant, and now I was finally a mother. My child was not just some random kid, either; I knew that she was truly special because a prophetess from my parents' church *said so* when I was pregnant. On that incredible day, the Prophetess Louella came over and placed her hands on my belly and had a *Word from the Lord* that my baby had been touched by God and was going to be very special indeed. Who could argue with a prophetess?

And my baby WAS very special – except for the colic. Her eardrum-piercing, high-pitched shrieking started at sundown every day and lasted for hours. Since I never slept more than 3 hours at a time (having to keep my Godly breastfeeding schedule), I struggled with irritability and lack of patience at times.

Herein lies an issue many fundamentalists have, which is that of only understanding the letter of the law. Because the parenting book stated that I was to adhere to a 3-hour schedule, I assumed that meant around the clock. In hindsight, I should not have woken my baby up through the night to feed her, but rather let her sleep as long as possible so that I could also get my rest and establish good sleep hygiene for her. As with most fundamentalists, however, nuance was beyond my grasp. The parenting book – my authority – instructed me to keep to a schedule, and it would have felt disobedient to break that rule.

Waking myself every 3 hours to feed our daughter, I became shaky from lack of sleep. I came to dread sundown, knowing my special baby would open her mouth and scream for hours on end. At that time, I would hand her over to her father. For the next several hours, he would wear her in a baby snugly and feed her gripe water (a nonprescription liquid supplement folk medicine thought to alleviate stomach pains) to try and soothe her. I had nothing more to give.

I prayed frequently for her colic to end, but my prayers went unanswered: Colic was with us for several months. I felt shrouded in failure that our baby was not perfectly serene and easy, and I wondered if the Prophetess Louella might have confused my baby with another Special Baby. I secretly hoped our daughter's crankiness did not indicate a willful temperament that would require severe discipline as she got older.

While I had previously worked many jobs, from cashier to receptionist, now that I was officially a SAHM (stay-at-home mom), we were forced to live on just one income. It would not do for a Christian mother to place her children in daycare for someone else to raise; it was much more respectable to attempt godly obedience in poverty. No longer a hairstylist, my husband worked extremely hard doing physical labor, applying stucco and plaster on the outside of homes. Paying our bills was a constant struggle, but we were always sure God had something better for us just around the corner. Or the next corner. Or maybe the next...

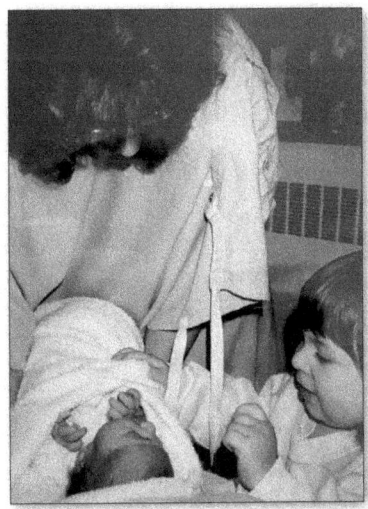

Big Sister meets Little Sister

Eventually, baby number 2 joined our family. At that point, my husband knew he had to decide on a better career path to support us. He determined that this would involve becoming a theology professor. I was thrilled with his vision, and he applied immediately to Prairie Bible Institute, a conservative Bible college in a small prairie town. He was accepted and applied for student loans to help pay the cost. Eventually, we made our way to the small town on the prairies that was to be our home for the next five years.

While my husband drove there, I was delighted to fly, since I had a 2-year-old and a newborn. My mother accompanied me, as I was still recovering from my Cesarean section. One thing concerned me about the flight: I was worried that landing would hurt our older daughter's ears, from the difference in air pressure. When I asked my doctor about this, she recommended offering our daughter her pacifier to suck on. As regimented as I had been about breastfeeding, I was equally regimented about my babies using pacifiers, generally only allowing them at nap time. Offering it to her in the middle of the day with no nap imminent was a definite change in my schedule.

As the plane began its descent and my toddler started tugging on her ear, I reached into the diaper bag and pulled out her beloved pacifier. "I know you only usually get this when you're going to sleep, but the doctor said it will help your ears feel better," I informed her, passing the rubber dummy to her little hand. Looking quizzical, she took the soother and promptly stuck it in her ear. She shook her head sadly at me, indicating it wasn't helping at all. I don't know who laughed harder, me or my mom; but I was going to miss that laughter in the days to come.

CHAPTER 4 LINKS & RESOURCES

CHAPTER FIVE

FUN(dy)TIMES AT BIBLE COLLEGE

We arrived in Three Hills, Alberta (really more like two hills and a bump) in January, taking up residence in the dilapidated mobile home we purchased in the married students' campus housing. We guessed it was built around 1950. It was small and barely insulated, with thick ice forming on the inside walls each winter. On the coldest days, we would hear glassware crack and break while it sat inside our kitchen cupboards.

Prairie Bible College, Alberta

Our vehicle was similarly inadequate for winter on the prairies. It was an old, uninsulated van that my husband had bought very cheaply. It took forever to warm up and was impossible to keep warm. On our first Sunday there we bundled up the children and elected to walk down to attend chapel, as it would take just as long to warm up the van. We walked all right, but we had nosebleeds by the time we got there from the bitter cold.

Sometime after my mother left us on our own in our new town, our youngest daughter (now about 2 months old) developed trouble breathing. I took her to the doctor, who said we needed to go to our town's "hospital" right away as she had RSV, a virus that can be serious for babies. They had trouble finding an oxygen mask small enough to fit her tiny face, and I was told to bring her back every four hours for treatment. In an actual hospital, I'm sure we could have just been admitted, but this place was far too small.

So, every four hours, I placed her in the pram and walked her back to receive oxygen therapy. I felt emotionally numb coping with a sick newborn in the dead of winter in a new town with only Mr. Spock for support. To make matters worse, our student loan was delayed, offering us a good taste of the poverty that would accompany us for the next 5 years as my husband attended Bible college in preparation for ministry. Never did it cross my mind to wonder why, when we were being so obedient to His will, God allowed our newborn to become dangerously ill, why I was married to an unfeeling husband, or why poverty seemed unshakable for us. Christians are taught to expect suffering and to bear it well, for the sake of the Gospel.

Though my body was still tired from surgery and now lack of sleep due to the new baby, I feared appearing lazy. Having been indoctrinated that a Christian woman should always be about her Heavenly Father's business, in addition to homemaking I became involved in the Student

Wives' Fellowship (eventually being named president). I also ran Story Time at the town library, seeing it as an opportunity to spread the Gospel.

Our Bible college was extremely active in preparing and sending out missionaries, training everyone from preachers to pilots to "Go out into all the world and preach the gospel" to heathens who were in desperate need of knowing they were going to Hell if they did not convert immediately to Christianity.

While we had no intention of becoming foreign missionaries, I made myself keenly aware of Christian persecution around the globe by subscribing to Voice of the Martyrs magazine. I also read regularly from Foxe's Book of Martyrs, introducing a slightly tamer version of it (produced by Christian rap group DC Talk) to my young daughters, wanting them to be fully prepared to lay down their lives for the Gospel should that day ever come. I now cringe over this recollection, seeing how grossly inappropriate it was to fill their innocent minds with fear of torture and death.

As an evangelical in the late 1990s, I felt it highly likely that either Muslims or atheists might one day take over the country and attack Christians, demanding that we renounce Christ or die. After all, it seemed like there were regular school shootings in the United States perpetrated by boys who had been brainwashed into the satanic Dungeons and Dragons cult; and according to the news, satanic worship (replete with human sacrifice) was on the rise. Yes, martyrdom seemed a real possibility in those days of Satanic Panic, and I was determined to prepare myself and my daughters.

Not wanting to be a lazy, lukewarm Christian, I developed a presentation for our Bible college's annual Missions Fest, focusing on the martyrdom of Christians around the world. I set up several tea light candles, which provided the only light source in the room. I ushered in attendees, urging them to be as quiet as possible so that our worship service would closely resemble one in underground China, for example.

With everyone sitting cross-legged on the floor, we (very quietly) sang hymns and recited Scripture from memory, since possessing either a Bible or a hymnal could be punishable by death. Every few minutes I blew out one candle, symbolizing a Christian life snuffed out by martyrdom in a hostile country. By the end, we were in a completely darkened room. It was a stupendously dramatic experience, from which many left in tears. We all felt inspired to pray harder, live holier, and prepare ourselves for our eventual martyrdom. Oh, the joy of life with a holy purpose!

DOWN THE FUNDY RABBIT HOLE

About our third year in the small Bible college town, I noticed the very modestly dressed women frequently shopping at our local grocery store. They always had their hair pinned up and worn beneath a fabric covering (also known as a head covering or veil). I was curious about this, as I had only seen women dressed like this in TV shows depicting Amish women. These ladies did not exactly look Amish, but they were definitely part of a religious group. After some inquiries, I learned that they belonged to a Mennonite sect called Holdeman Mennonites, or Church of God in Christ Mennonites, and they lived on farms just outside of town.

I decided to investigate the Bible for any admonitions regarding women's dress, not wanting to be disobedient to Scripture in any way. I knew the Old Testament rules no longer applied (such as offering animal sacrifice to receive forgiveness) because Jesus came to fulfill those Old Testament laws – but anything in the *New* Testament should still be observed.

To my astonishment, there were rules prescribing proper dress and adornment for women found in the New Testament, including these:

- ✠ Outward adornment was bad. No fancy hairdos, jewelry, or fine clothes (1 Peter 3:2-4)

- ✠ Praying or prophesying with an uncovered head was disgraceful, as was a woman with short hair (1 Corinthians 11:5)

- ✠ Women were to remain silent in church and be in submission to men. It was disgraceful for women to speak in church (1 Cor 14:33-35)

Additionally, a verse existed further confirming the undercurrents of what I'd picked up on in my family of origin. This verse stated that men were a reflection of God Himself, but women were a mere reflection of men (1 Corinthians 11:4-7).

While some interpreted these verses to mean women only needed to wear head coverings during times of prayer, I knew there was also a verse commanding all Christians to pray without ceasing (1 Thessalonians 5:16-17); hence, an attitude of prayer was desirable at all times.

To me, this meant that my hair needed to be as long as possible and always covered, other than when sleeping or bathing. With my husband's permission, I immediately adopted head-covering, or veiling, as a visible symbol and reminder to myself that my husband was to be my spiritual head and the boss of our family.

While I had previously given up playing guitar and writing in order not to "outshine" my husband, it was at this point that I earnestly tried to become less so that my heavenly Father could shine more brightly through me without worldly distractions. I also worked hard to tame my tongue, neither questioning, talking back, nor offering my opinion, to my husband. Though I was never rude in our discussions, this extent of forced submission and self-monitoring did not come naturally to me.

Happy with more rules to follow, I removed my wedding ring, put it away with all my other jewelry, and got rid of my makeup. With my glue gun and some fabric, I started making coverings for my hair, until I could order some "proper" ones courtesy of the holy ladies at the *She Maketh Herself Coverings* online boutique.

Striving to be the best at humility, I didn't want photos taken of me during my time of "veiling," so only a few exist, which I provide here as proof of my extreme fundamentalism.

My first holy head covering, thanks to my godly glue gun

Mesh snood head covering

Reminiscent of the Middle Ages, snoods were brought back to popularity during Victorian times. Failing to thoroughly cover my hair, this mesh snood was more like a glorified hair net from a fast-food kitchen.

The reason for my big smile is that Billy Graham's *Decision Magazine* had just accepted my testimony to be included as a feature piece.

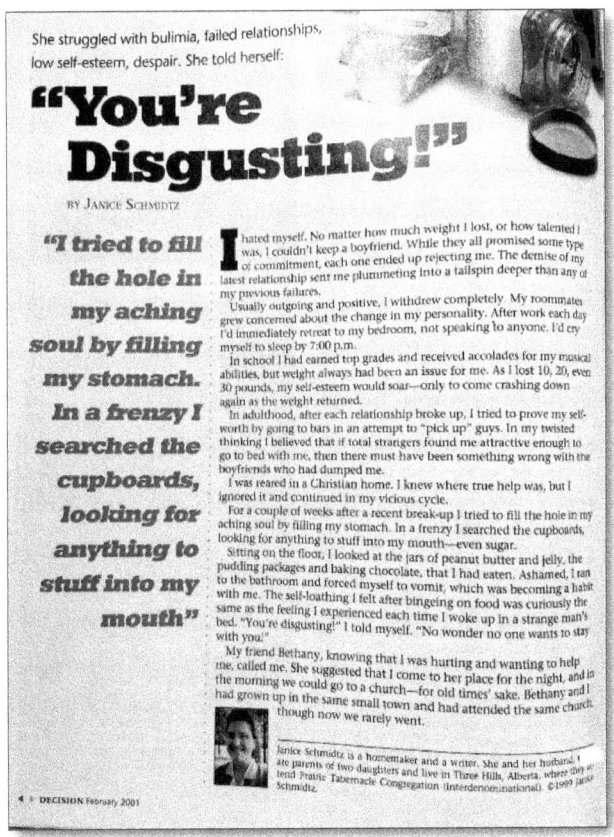

That time when I was a Billy Graham centerfold
(Decision Vol. 42, No. 2, February 2001)

Fabric-lined snood head covering

Realizing that the mesh snood was subpar when it came to the serious matter of feminine holiness, I decided they needed to be lined with fabric, as in the above photo.

In the end, though, nothing quite screamed "Behold my holy obedience" like the white hanky version of head coverings. Oh, my sanctified bliss!

Ever the concerned Christian mother, I felt convicted by the Holy Ghost that my daughters should likewise not have short hair. Until attending schools that had regular lice epidemics, they both kept waist-length hair.

Not content with merely covering my hair, I tossed out all my pants, shorts, and even culottes in favour of long skirts, dresses, and rompers. I also felt it improper for my daughters to wear pants, other than snow pants, so they required new clothing as well. The number of trips made to local thrift stores during that time was dizzying.

Behold: My rule-loving, head-covering, trying-to-be-submissive, wishing-I-was-a-Holdeman-Mennonite self.

Admiring my own spiritual growth, I took to calling myself a *Mennocostal*, as I believed that I had successfully managed to combine both the holy, plain living of the closed Mennonites with the vibrance of Pentecostalism that was so precious to me. Moved to model my obedience, I thus presented myself to the world – and the rest of the student body at Prairie Bible College – as *The Lord's Veiled Handmaid*. While I cringe about it now, that's how I began signing my correspondence. No one loved the letter of the law more than I did, and now everyone would know.

Out went TV, secular radio, and any other worldly influences. In came Focus on the Family (along with all things James Dobson) and Bill Gothard (with his Advanced Training Institute and Basic Life Principles). Barring my few "backslidden years" between ages 18 to 21, it was when

I started wearing a head covering and long dresses that my identity became *completely* enmeshed with my beliefs.

During this period, I emulated my plain sisters by becoming a pacifist and refusing to vote. Though I did not express it, my refusal to vote was less about pacifism and more about doubting whether women should even be able to vote, since they were inferior to men. I took the Bible so seriously that I even wondered if women should have driver's licenses. Rather than holding my faith, it was now holding me. I was becoming more and more radicalized.

I remember one uncomfortable conversation from this time that still makes me cringe. An old friend of my then-husband called to tell us that she was getting remarried, having previously divorced. I "felt led" to point out to her that, not only does God hate divorce, but the New Testament plainly condemns remarriage - so we could not support her new marriage. This poor woman had already been through so much, and I poured more salt into her wounds, believing it was the holy thing to do. I *hate* that I did this.

Believing that my head covering gave me better heavenly reception, I felt confident to act any time the Holy Spirit moved me to do so. One morning, I attended chapel in my husband's place while he slept in... er... watched the children. As usual, I loved the praise and worship time and settled in to learn from whatever godly man might be teaching us today. Only it wasn't a man at all. It was a trim young woman WEARING A SATIN PANTSUIT! I don't remember anything she said on stage, but I sure do remember her curvy figure in that pantsuit. It looked to me like the young men in front of me were also paying extremely close attention to every move she made.

Certain that she would want to soak up the godly wisdom of an older, holier woman, I tapped her on the shoulder after she sat down. I thanked her for coming to our college but wanted her to know that much of what she said was likely not heard by the men in the chapel over the *roar* of her hip-hugging, sexy satin pantsuit. I encouraged her, in the future, to dress more modestly so she would not be guilty of causing a brother to stumble. I am cringing at this memory. *Dear Lady, if by any chance you read this book and recognize our interaction, please excuse me for what I said as a brainwashed Mennocostal.*

Though I did not try to convert strangers, I welcomed every opportunity to talk about my faith if they approached me – and they did. I recall one time in a Christian bookstore when a stranger insisted on buying me a book about Christian mystics, and another time an elderly husband and wife we'd never met paid for our dinner with the kids at a family restaurant. I attribute these events, at least in part, to the visibility of my head covering.

My husband was more of an introvert and not overly comfortable with the changes I was making, as they forced him into a position of authority and decision-making that felt unnatural to him. Ironically, I told myself that I was making those very changes to help me be a better, more submissive, wife. This was a peculiar pattern I observed in other ultra-conservative families through the years, with quiet husbands and not-so-quiet wives who seemed desperate to present a picture-perfect image of a "biblical" family.

SOPHIA ACADEMY

By this time, our eldest daughter was ready to start school. Homeschooling was the only option I considered, as it would allow me to provide her with a superior education while saving her from worldly contamination. Accordingly, I took up the mantle of homeschool teacher. Our tiny school was thoughtfully named Sophia Academy since Sophia means *wisdom* in Greek, and my husband was desperately trying to learn that ancient language as part of his biblical studies.

After borrowing a friend's Abeka Christian curriculum to teach our oldest how to read, I decided to teach using the trivium method of instruction. In classical education, the trivium is a set of three phases: Grammar, logic, and rhetoric. This is supposed to help children first learn knowledge, then understanding, and finally, wisdom. In modern times, it has fallen into disuse because so many more subjects are available to be taught.

Daughter number 1 (the prototype) was a sponge for knowledge, and teaching her was a sheer delight. Eager to learn, obey, and please, she was a Christian mother's dream. I confess to feeling a fulfillment with homeschooling that I did not feel with motherhood alone. I not only had a purpose, but my results were measurable. I was training our daughters in holiness *and* academics. Daughter number 2, however, was somewhat less thrilled about the idea of being forced to learn anything—especially at home.

Raising kids with a partner who seemed neurodivergent meant that I laughed or cried a good deal of the time. I chose laughter whenever possible. My ex-husband is exceptionally bright in some areas and completely lost in others. I recall coming home from an evening out at the Student Wives' Fellowship gathering, to an eerily silent home. A single clue had been left for me in the laundry room/entry: A huge pile of powdered laundry soap was standing in the middle of the room, minus the bucket it came in.

Instantly, I knew that one or both children had ingested some of the soap while their dad was "watching" them, and he had taken both girls and the bucket to our little urgent care clinic to make sure they would be okay after eating the soap. This was in the days before mobile phones, but my mother's intuition was spot-on. A couple of hours later they returned home, and their exciting tale confirmed my suspicions. On another occasion, it was motor oil that the 3-year-old thought the

2-year-old might like to drink while Dad let them play (again, he was "watching" them) in the family van.

One final, more humorous example was when our youngest sneezed, and fluorescent yellow goo flew out of her nose. When Husband heard me shriek in surprise over the unnatural color, he ran to his den and returned with a highlighter – minus the nib, which Daughter had ingested (of course, during a time he was "babysitting" her).

Our marriage could be incredibly frustrating. While deeply intelligent in specific technical areas, he was extremely distant emotionally. Only years later did he express his frustration that he couldn't seem to be the type of partner I wanted, feeling that I was never satisfied. And in some ways, he was right; I was never emotionally satisfied with our partnership. It often felt like I was married to a robot. I felt that I had to be both mother and father to our children, as his mind was always somewhere else. His nicknames amongst those who knew him at the Bible College were Spock and the Absent-Minded Professor.

LIFE WITH THE ABSENT-MINDED PROFESSOR

One example of this still makes me laugh and roll my eyes. As all Junior-year students at the Bible college were expected to help out with Senior-year activities, my husband ended up on a decorating committee. After a meeting one evening, he pulled out a crumpled piece of paper from his pocket and tossed it on our dining table.

"What's this for?" I asked, opening it to see a Bible verse scrawled in his poor penmanship. He replied that his job on the committee was to write out that particular Bible verse for the Seniors. Knowing his propensity for missing details, I quizzed him for more information. He shrugged his shoulders and stated he hadn't missed anything: His job was just to write out that verse, so he did.

Still suspicious, I suggested making it into an art project for our eldest daughter, now about age 7. I had her cut up strips of colored construction paper into small squares we would glue onto a piece of poster board, making a mosaic in the style of ancient Rome. Together, we diligently worked on the project for a couple of weeks. In the end, I used my best calligraphy skills to write out the verse, now flanked by a colorful mosaic of various fruits.

Soon after, all families were called to an evening assembly to celebrate the graduating class. On stage, a floor-length velvet curtain hid the lectern, creating an air of mystery. To our utter astonishment, the President of the Bible college pulled back the curtain to reveal *our* art project, matted and framed behind glass, which would be hung in the administration office to represent the graduating class! My jaw dropped as my husband looked sheepishly at the floor. At home later, he sighed and said, "I guess you were right," which was the closest I would get to either thanks or an apology. When I visited the college over a decade later, our artwork was still on display for all to see.

While I took joy in being a homemaker and a homeschool mom, the main feeling I had regarding our union was one of intense frustration. We were speaking different languages, and it was nobody's fault. Unfortunately, as Christian women are trained to do, I perceived our difficulties were due solely to my flaws because I was not subservient or meek enough. God Himself had provided my husband to me to be "my spiritual head." There was no way our problems could be his fault. Ironically, one of the main reasons I wore a head covering was to remind myself that I needed to submit, Submit, SUBMIT!

Eventually, my husband's student loans were cut off. His work doing stucco and plaster around the college town would not be enough to keep him in school and pay for our household needs, and my returning to the workforce was certainly not a holy enough option. To my horror, he decided that he would have to give up on his dreams of becoming a professor and instead *seek work as a pastor*. Panic rose within me as I knew what a terrible mistake that would be.

A pastor must also be a shepherd, gentle and loving with his flock – not a robotic man oblivious to social norms. I begged and pleaded on my knees for him not to put our family through what I suspected would be an agonizing move. My tearful pleading seemed only to harden his resolve, prompting his cold response: "Someone has to steer this boat, and that person is me." This was the time he chose to assert his male headship as the head of our Christian home – and it proved disastrous.

CHAPTER 5 LINKS & RESOURCES

CHAPTER SIX

THE PASTOR DISASTER

We left the next morning for his new pastoral job. His lack of attention to detail and unwillingness to listen while packing our things resulted in significant damage to family heirlooms – just another casualty of life with my oblivious Spiritual Head. Though furious with my husband, I did my best to put a positive spin on things for our young daughters by telling them we were headed for adventure in a brand-new province they had never seen.

I realized I may have over-emphasized this point when we pulled into a diner after crossing the provincial border and our daughter excitedly asked: "How did I understand our waitress? Do they speak English here?"

Our new town had fewer than 1,000 residents, and our new church had only about 25 members, mostly senior citizens. I learned quickly that the two least popular families in small Canadian towns are those of the minister and the police. Town residents know that neither of these families is likely to set down roots in their community because as soon as a better opportunity arises, they will take it and leave.

Unbeknownst to me, my husband had privately assured the church board that we would stay for four years, regardless of anything that might come up. When he finally disclosed this to me, I felt sick to my stomach.

HOW (NOT) TO SAVE A DYING CHURCH

It has been said that the last words of a dying church are *"But we don't do things that way!"* In our case, that certainly rang true. I learned quickly that the congregation had strong feelings about how things were to be done (or *not* done). Our congregants were mostly elderly farmers who simply wanted to be comforted as they aged and prepared to meet their Maker. They were not interested in changing anything and deeply resented the changes that were being forced on them.

The first change was the worship music: Out went cherished old hymns played on the baby grand piano, and in came drums and electric guitars complete with giant speaker stacks for the hard of hearing. If they weren't struggling with hearing loss when we arrived, I'm certain they were when we departed. Their new pastor updated the music with gusto, refusing to allow more than one hymn per week.

My husband also determined it was time to change the name of the church. Nothing was to be spared in our attempts to keep the church from dying off completely. The name we decided on was a complete oxymoron: New Life Church.

It was during this challenging year that I learned something helpful: I found out about Autism Spectrum Disorder (ASD). Once I learned about the autism spectrum, I asked my husband if he was willing to take some online tests to see if he might be on the spectrum. When he scored extremely high, things started to make a lot more sense. It gave me a broader perspective of my spouse.

Previously, I figured he was just trying to be a jerk; but now, I recognized that he was often actually doing his best to try and navigate the NT (neurotypical) world of those not on the spectrum. This placed him at a significant disadvantage relationally, because some ND (neurodivergent) folk can struggle to pick up on social cues. Learning this explained his consistent and sometimes comical social blunders, like earlier asking the young woman if she was pregnant and another woman if she dyed her hair.

In our new community, one of his faux pas was the habit of locking the church doors during his office hours. My husband was in love with his job and did not want anyone to disturb him while he worked on sermons. As you might imagine, the parishioners did not take kindly to being locked out of their own church.

When I reported to my husband that church elders were asking me to get him to slow the rate of change he was forcing on our congregation, he replied that the problem was with my wearing a head covering. He felt it caused too much division between me and the other church ladies and demanded that I stop wearing it. This caused me deep sorrow, as I genuinely thought I was being obedient to scripture and needed the additional help to submit to him - but I dutifully removed my covering.

To try and increase Sunday attendance, Pastor Husband decided to organize a youth group. Every Wednesday night teens came to our Pentecostal church to watch episodes of The Simpsons, following which he would give a short talk trying to relate lessons from the show to Bible parables. For my part, I asked two other church ladies to help me organize and run a Kids Club after school every Friday. Parents in town were thrilled to have free childcare on Friday afternoons as we did our best to indoctrinate their children.

During that year, I did things I hadn't thought I would do. I allowed both of our daughters to attend the town (public) school, at least part-time; volunteered at the local curling/skating rink; coached peewee soccer (during which I allowed myself to wear pants, feeling they would be more modest than running around the field in a long dress); and submitted articles to the local newspaper. All these activities were my attempts to weave our family (and church) into the community. As usual, my Spiritual Head failed to notice the efforts I was making.

WHAT'S A WIFE TO DO?

I was trying my hardest to be a good pastor's wife. I even tried to keep my complaining to a minimum when, instead of money to help pay my husband's salary, some farmers instead tithed with green beans and potatoes. Though I desperately lacked a green thumb, I had even gone so far as spending days weeding a portion of the parsonage backyard so that I could plant a few seeds. Disappointingly, ladies in the congregation chose to disparage my efforts and shame my gardening ignorance rather than show me what to do.

Not feeling I was making adequate headway in our new town, I determined that what we needed was a modern coffee shop; a cool place for teens to gather in the evenings and for all residents to enjoy. Christians recognize this as "tent-making," operating a business for the sake of proselytizing. Looking back, I also see that it was my entrepreneurial spirit trying to break through.

I polled moms at the skating rink to find out what they would like in such a space, asked strangers for name ideas, and even approached the town for financial aid in getting my business off the ground. For the first time since our arrival, I started feeling some excitement at the thought that maybe I really could make a difference in this dying prairie town.

I was thrilled when the time came for me to scope out local real estate for what I had decided to call the Little Stone Coffee Shop. I asked my husband to accompany me, feeling it appropriate to include my Spiritual Head in this business decision. Unfortunately, he talked to the realtor about everything except renting the space. I felt myself growing frustrated and finally tentatively broke into their conversation to ask a question pertinent to our visit.

To my horror, my husband chastised me for interrupting their conversation. My face grew hot and red with humiliation and anger. I apologized and quietly left, walking home on my own. By now, my cheeks were familiar with the hot tears streaming down them.

CRACKS IN THE FACADE

While blow-ups between us were rare, this experience immediately brought to mind another event that left me writhing in emotional pain back on the Bible college campus. After what I thought had been an enjoyable evening entertaining dinner guests in our home, my husband chastised me for talking too much.

Another time, I asked him to help me clear the table and he asked why. When I told him it would set a good example for our daughters to see their daddy helping with housework, he coldly replied that *it would set a better example for their mommy to do so with a servant's heart* (i.e., with a quiet and gentle spirit). My breath caught in my throat as he turned and walked out of the room. While such episodes were out of character for my generally easy-going husband, each one stung as though he had slapped me in the face.

Within a few days of the humiliating incident with the realtor, my husband told me that I was to stop my efforts to open the coffee shop. He was too frustrated with the church board opposing what he felt was Divinely inspired change. Following Matthew 10:14, he was preparing to shake the dust off his feet, leaving the church and town altogether. When I reminded him of his four-year promise to them, he told me the promise did not count since the church refused to modernize. He did not want to be known as the pastor whose church died. I asked him to consider slowing down the rate of change he was making, but he was resolute in his decision. While disappointed that I wouldn't be able to open my shop, I confess I felt a certain happiness at the thought of leaving.

THE BEGINNING OF THE END

On one of the final Sundays in our tiny church, I was on stage in my usual position - attempting to lead the congregation in the worship music they now despised. Many parishioners sat with their mouths clenched shut and their arms crossed in front of them. None of them knew the personal burdens I was carrying. Years in a difficult marriage had been capped with an intensely challenging year trying to support my (suspected) neurodivergent husband who was poorly suited to pastoring. Additionally, my parents had separated after over 40 years of marriage, and my teenage nephew had stabbed a man to death back home and was now a fugitive. The police informed me that I was to contact them immediately if I heard from my nephew.

Looking out over the hostile congregation of farmers with their arms crossed and mouths shut rather than participating in praise and worship time, I reached my breaking point. I stopped singing mid-song, tears streaming down my face. Clipping my microphone back on its stand, I walked down the aisle to the foyer. Silently, I turned and walked downstairs to the basement, where my quiet sobs could not be heard. No one followed.

That day my husband had decided to preach a strong sermon against "the sins of the flesh," and at times he was graphic. "Too graphic," I had warned him when he informed me of his sermon plans, but he felt the elderly congregants had to be made aware of what sins were transpiring all over the world. From my lonely and tearful spot in the church basement, I occasionally heard footsteps and doors closing as a few couples were so offended by his colorful message that they got up and left mid-service. No one came downstairs to check on me. I waited until the service was over and everyone had left, then I walked home alone.

GOODBYE PASTOR, HELLO PLASTER

Soon after that sad Sunday, we were on the road again, heading back to Alberta. This time we were aiming for Calgary, a city of about a million people at that time. Our daughters were wide-eyed when I explained to them that as many people lived in our new apartment building in Calgary as lived in our entire former town in Saskatchewan. We enrolled the children in a good public school nearby and I began an online course learning medical transcription (even though my in-laws were convinced it was a scam) since my husband's income in construction would not be enough to support us in the city.

Unfortunately, our new location did not help my husband's mood. He plunged into a deep depression tinged with anger, blaming me for the loss of his dreams. While I was significantly happier not having to constantly extinguish the social fires he unintentionally set with our former congregation, he deeply lamented the loss of a job that had been so meaningful to him. We spent our time arguing or in cold silence. Returning to the construction trade he hated made him feel like a total failure.

My folks were delighted that we were closer to home, though still a full day's drive away. With Mom and Dad now separated, Mom and I plotted about how we might move back to our hometown and possibly buy a house with an in-law suite for her to live in. While we researched realty possibilities, my husband was not impressed and continued to blame me for his losses.

During that time, I finally attended a dentist to have my teeth cleaned. It had been about seven years since I'd seen a dentist, as we just never had the money for it (dentistry is not covered by Canadian healthcare). To my embarrassment, it was while I was recumbent in the dental chair, a stranger scraping my teeth, that the tears of anger, frustration, and sadness over my marriage decided to flow. As the Greek poet Sappho noted centuries earlier: "What cannot be said will be wept."

Though my mother found a house that would have suited our purposes, my Spiritual Head refused to move back directly to our hometown and decided instead to take a job in a community about 2 hours away. This job involved us moving into the home of the man he would be working for, essentially out in the forest. While I wasn't especially thrilled to be moving our family in with a stranger, I was happy to be inching closer to my mother, our friends, and our home church community. Once again, we loaded up kids and cat and moved to a new location.

My husband's new employer was eccentric, to say the least. He was a divorced fellow in his 40s who claimed to be a Christian. His nearly 5,000 square foot house in the woods was unfinished. The location was picturesque, but something felt off to me. When we heard murmurings from some of the townsfolk that our landlord was not entirely trustworthy, I decided to check in with the local police to learn anything I should know. They were familiar with him but assured me he posed no known threat to children if that was my concern.

Things got weirder as our new landlord took a shine to me. One day, he took me and my youngest daughter for a walk along one of his newly acquired properties and commented that he would be happy to step in and help raise our kids should my husband die in an accident. When I shared this with my husband, he was merely amused. In fact, he was not even remotely concerned - until he stopped getting paid for his work.

Tensions arose in our shared home around payment disputes, and we felt relieved when our landlord/boss told us he would be leaving soon for a fishing trip. A couple of nights before he was to leave, we could not find our indoor cat. The next morning, I was horrified to see her looking bedraggled outside the glass door to our patio. When I let her in, she shot to the bedroom and hid beneath our bed. She wheezed heavily and refused to budge for hours, leading us to think she might not survive. Eventually, she peered out and let us pick her up.

I immediately took her to the vet, who noted ligature marks around her paws and felt that our beloved cat had been tied up and abused. When I cried to the vet that I was worried about our landlord, he immediately asked if we were living with Mr. _____. When I answered affirmatively, he gave me his business card and included his home phone number, emphatically stating that we were not safe and needed to move out as soon as possible. I was in shock.

The next day was the day our landlord was leaving, and it happened to also be our youngest daughter's birthday. We had a party planned for her with several schoolmates in our home. After my conversation with the vet, however, we knew we couldn't stay. I called our daughters' godparents, from our hometown, and they dutifully showed up after our landlord left and helped us pack all of our things. We went ahead with the birthday party which also turned out to be a goodbye party.

I called our old pastor, the one who had introduced and married us, and asked if he knew of any place we might rent. As it happened, half of the duplex he owned and lived in with his wife was vacant. He immediately offered it to us, and we felt very relieved to have a safe place to move to. Our daughters were scared and surprised by our sudden departure. We left no forwarding address, as we felt it unsafe to do so.

HOMEWARD BOUND

Finally, after nearly a decade away from my parents, our friends, and my hometown, we were moving home! I was overjoyed by this turn of events, but my husband was still vexed and blamed me for his continued misery. I hoped that we might finally get to settle down, lick our wounds, and adjust to our new course.

I took a job doing medical transcription at our local hospital soon after we moved back. I showed up daily in long skirts and modest blouses, with my long hair. While it felt odd being away from home all day and I was unsure what it would be like working with so many heathen women, I came to love my coworkers. I soon resumed wearing pants and makeup.

At the mall with a Christian friend who never succumbed to the extremes I had clung to, I bought my first pair of earrings in many years. I smiled at myself in the mirror and my friend cheered me on as I continued my reintegration process back into the regular world. The suffocating grip of fundamentalism was losing its hold on me.

The hospital required banking information for the direct deposit of my paycheques. My husband and I had shared a bank account and had only his credit card throughout our marriage. While he never asked me to do so, I had canceled my credit cards just before our wedding, thinking it improper for a wife to have her own. Now, though, when the opportunity arose for me to have my own bank account, I pounced on it.

While I could not bring myself to say it aloud, I was pining for independence and preparing for my departure. When I informed him that I had opened an account, he was angry and hurt. He had always put all his money into our joint account. Why wasn't I willing to do the same? I knew it was not the right time to inform him that I had also applied for my own credit card.

FROM BAD TO WORSE

While I was somewhat hopeful things would improve, the calamities kept coming. Taking stock of all that had transpired within two years was breathtaking: My parents divorced, my young nephew went to prison for killing a stranger, we entered and exited the pastorate and moved four times. Sadly, the most painful event was yet to come.

After moving back to our hometown, our youngest daughter's health began to fail. Over about six months, she lost weight, experienced blurred vision, had horrifying stomach pain and sweet-smelling breath, and felt an unquenchable thirst. I took her to our family doctor, then to a pediatrician, and also made various trips to the ER - each time telling them that I suspected she had Type 1 Diabetes. In a prime example of doctors writing off a mother as histrionic and compulsively worried, they told me that she was simply having a growth spurt and that her eye issues were related, somehow, to asthma.

Finally, at 2 o'clock one morning, I heard her rattling around in the kitchen. She informed me that she was opening her *third* bottle of water that night. In that instant, I knew without a doubt that the doctors were wrong. I woke my husband and told him that the next morning I was taking her to a walk-in clinic to see a doctor who didn't know us and that I was not going to offer my thoughts on her symptoms. I told my husband to expect an afternoon call telling him she had diabetes.

The next morning, I kept her home from school and took her to see a doctor we didn't know. He examined her and then stepped out of the office for several minutes. When he returned, he told us we were to go straight to the hospital, not even stopping at home for an overnight bag. He sadly informed us that my daughter had Type 1 Diabetes and that her extremely high blood sugar put her in significant danger. He had called ahead to the hospital, and they were expecting us.

With tears blurring my vision, I drove my sweet little girl to the hospital. I nearly broke down when she said: "Don't worry, Mom! I can handle anything... as long as I don't have to get a needle!" She had no idea that needles were going to become a daily, sometimes hourly, part of her life.

I called my husband from the hospital, and he picked up our older daughter to bring her in. We spent the next hours learning how to use a finger-tip poker to test blood sugar and how to inject insulin into an orange before each of us took a turn injecting our precious family member with the life-saving nectar of insulin. I roomed in with our daughter for the next week on the Pediatric floor, doing my best to learn how to navigate this cruel and complicated disease.

Within a few months of our daughter's diagnosis, my husband informed me that we were falling too far behind on our bills, even with both of us working. Medical care is covered in Canada but not medication, insulin pumps, or blood glucose testing kits. He said that his only option was to declare bankruptcy, have the debts wiped out, and lose our credit for seven years - after which, we could start rebuilding our credit again.

My head was spinning. I had been raised to view bankruptcy as a significant character flaw, to say the least. It was shirking one's responsibility, something lazy people did; it was practically a *sin*. A Christian had no business declaring bankruptcy. Wouldn't God provide for us in our time of need? I begged my husband to have more faith or find another way. Truthfully, we had no assets to sell. We did not own a home or a new car. Rent was high, groceries and medication were costly, and his student loan payments put us over the top. We were drowning, and bankruptcy was going to be our life preserver.

Enduring this series of calamities left our marriage hanging by a thread.

CHAPTER 6 LINKS & RESOURCES

CHAPTER SEVEN

MY EXTIMONY: WHY I LEFT CHRISTIANITY

Entreating God for relief from our calamitous onslaught was met with silence. I was the recipient of both the judgment and fear that fundamentalist Christians inadvertently dish out while trying to cover their own cognitive dissonance: *What possible sin had I committed to merit God's divine punishment?*

While I frantically reviewed my life looking for the answer, I could not find anything worthy of Him afflicting my innocent child with a deadly disease. Christian friends told me to pray more and also to fast (refrain from food) for God to see my earnestness. If God was not moved by my river of tears, I doubted fasting would help. My life and marriage were falling apart, and now my precious child was suffering.

My faith was now officially under deconstruction.

I didn't feel that I could discuss my doubts with my husband, though he was no longer attending church. Adding to my frustration, he now spent most of his spare time in the basement playing the new multiplayer video game *World of Warcraft* (Blizzard Entertainment; November 23, 2004; World of Warcraft; Shane Dabiri, Carlos Guerrero). Frequently awakening alone at night to find him online downstairs, it felt like the video game was his mistress. I wept bitter tears, feeling abandoned by both God and my husband.

Looking back, I see that it was simply my husband's way of seeking an escape from the pressures of life. Feeling as though he was being beaten to a pulp despite his best efforts, he needed to feel powerful somewhere —and that place was in the make-believe video game world. Unfortunately, our daughters also noticed his increasing absence. I remember one evening taking our car out and considering my options. I wanted to drive and drive and never go home. My thoughts became increasingly desperate as the days wore on with no emotional relief in sight.

My life was unraveling before my eyes, and I was powerless to stop it. If you have never had a child with a life-threatening illness, you can't fully understand the despair I felt as a parent helpless to comfort my child. Battling that while at the same time losing my faith made my despair that much darker. What if my child died and no heaven existed for her? What if my disbelief condemned my children to go to Hell (Exodus 20:5 and 34:7)? Fear and sadness threatened to suffocate me.

ACoRNS: CHRISTIAN CODEPENDENCY

We attended a religious counsellor for a time (paid for by the church) in an attempt to help save our marriage. After only a couple of visits, my husband declared it useless because "all we do is talk." I attended a few more times on my own during which the counsellor introduced me to the idea of codependency. At first, I was offended and told her I didn't think that described our situation; but eventually, I came to see that it was entirely true.

Codependency can be described roughly as a relationship dynamic where one person assumes the role of being the "giver" (sacrificing their own needs and well-being) and the other adopts the role of the "taker."

Rather than a diagnosis or a personality disorder, codependency is a relational dynamic where the couple slips into a state of over- and under-functioning. It is an unhealthy coping tactic that some have described as "the need to be needed." Passive-aggressive communication can easily become a habit in codependent relationships, rather than each partner sharing truthfully about their feelings and concerns.

Those who grow up in families with a parent who suffers from substance addiction are known as ACoA or Adult Children of Alcoholics. Since we share many of the characteristics of ACoA, I call those of us who grew up with parents addicted to religious ideology ACoRNs: Adult Children of Religious Nuts.

In my case, it was hard to determine which challenges were from my family of origin, which were from religious views of marriage, and which arose from being a neurotypical woman married to a likely neurodivergent man. Learning about codependency was interesting and somewhat insightful, but (like learning about Autism Spectrum Disorder), it wasn't overly helpful.

UNCOMFORTABLY NUMB: GRIEF

The pressure became too great; I had to find a way to alleviate it. My marriage was quickly unraveling and I could not face the pain of possibly also losing my daughter to her illness. I started to formulate a plan that involved hoarding painkillers to overdose. The thought of being free from my emotional pain was very enticing. I could just take pills and never wake up again. No more marital woes, no more crushing poverty, no more fear.

Fortunately, in a moment of clarity, I realized I had to get help. My children needed me – but I felt weak and confused. I went to a walk-in clinic to see a doctor, pulling a baseball cap down low over my face so as not to be recognized by anyone I might know in the clinic. I felt exhausted and could not bring myself to look at the receptionist in the face.

Soon I was sitting in the doctor's office, recounting the many recent disappointments, frustrations, and burdens. She asked me if I could think of even one reason why I should not kill myself. "My kids," I replied. The doctor heaved a sigh of relief and handed me a piece of paper. "This is a safety contract," she explained. I signed the agreement not to harm myself. She told me I was not to go home, where I would be alone. I agreed I could go over to my mother's place and spend a few hours with her. The doctor asked for my mother's phone number and released me to my mother's care.

Within half an hour of being at Mom's place, the phone rang. Mom looked quizzical as she handed me the phone. A mental health worker was on the other end of the line. My doctor had contacted them and told them I needed a mental health check-in. The worker asked me about my suicide plan and if I would be willing to give my painkillers and other potentially toxic medications either to a trusted friend or return them to the pharmacy. I agreed with this plan.

At that point, I was beyond praying. The lack of having my prayers answered was partly what drove me to thoughts of suicide. I recognized that my religious beliefs were misguided, and even started to question the existence of God at all. I saw that the man I married was not the right partner for me, and we would not have married had it not been for our religion. Prayer was not helping me, my marriage, or my daughter; regardless of how fervently and sincerely my petitions were made.

I didn't know that I was grieving not only the dissolution of my marriage but my entire worldview. One late night I found myself alone in the living room watching an old black and white war movie. The hero had escaped his prison camp along with a few others. One by one, they died of snipers, starvation, and poisonous snake bites. Eventually, he was alone in the jungle, not knowing which way to go. Tears streamed down his face as he shook his fist up at the full moon and yelled "I don't even believe in You anymore!" Tears streamed down my face as I stared up at the full moon outside my living room window, feeling utterly abandoned and completely lost. "I don't even believe in You anymore" echoed in my heart.

At that point, I knew no one else who had been as devout as me who had turned away from God. I instinctively knew that others could not understand my losses or the profound depth of my grief. Later on, I would learn that the name for my loss was *ambiguous loss* because there was no body to bury. Additionally, my grief was both *disenfranchised grief* - because it was not understood or socially sanctioned – and *unresolved grief* because it was without closure and cumulative. I felt certain that I was not just "backsliding."

For me, Christianity was circling the drain. To my consternation, my absence from church services went largely unnoticed, with only a couple of people bothering to call me and check up. One warned me that I was on a perilous path and likely sending my children to Hell. Mostly, though, the silence was deafening.

I couldn't believe the callousness of my church family, especially considering our daughter's serious diagnosis. This betrayal felt significant. I believed I was an important member of my church community. Wherever I lived, I had poured hours into my local church serving on committees, worship teams, or in the nursery. How could so few people notice or care about my departure? Today, I know that Believers often shy away from questioning those who leave because they fear apostasy may be contagious – but at the time, I took it very personally.

In addition to struggling with suicidal thoughts, I felt shocked, angry, confused, betrayed, numb, and vulnerable. Never in a million years would I have believed that I could lose my faith. I sometimes cried uncontrollably, becoming overwhelmed by small things. I lost my appetite and became forgetful. I experienced throat tightness; headaches; and frequently heaved deep, mournful sighs. When my daughters asked if I was okay, I told them I was just tired. Now, I recognize all of these as signs of grief and mourning. The victim was my faith, and the murderer was reality.

I tried once or twice more to attend church services, but the songs about God's faithfulness turned to sawdust in my mouth, and I had to leave before my facial floodgates opened again. I realized that the God I had served was either uncaring or nonexistent, and I could offer worship no longer. I was experiencing a truth spoken by Emerson over a century earlier: "The mind, once stretched by a new idea, never returns to its original dimensions." For me, there would be no turning back.

I felt unmoored, like a grey dinghy afloat on a grey ocean surrounded by a grey fog. My once-firm guideposts dissolved, around me and within me. The world became topsy-turvy, and nothing made sense. I no longer had hooks – or even walls - on which to orderly hang the beliefs of my formerly protective assumptive worldview.

It was the strangest feeling *not* to pray. Sometimes I had to fight the urge. Through every other crisis of my life, prayer had played a daily, sometimes hourly, role. Praying felt like it kept me connected to God, like it was necessary to keep him from forgetting how much I needed Him. But I was no longer willing to beg at God's table for crumbs of grace or an indication that He might exist or care about me. My "relationship" with God was now giving me *abusive boyfriend* vibes, since He refused to acknowledge me yet threatened to torture me if I left. Likewise, a vague sense of Stockholm Syndrome was floating around the periphery of my mind. *For an article on Divine Trauma Bonding, see Chapter 7 Resources.*

Losing my Cosmic Big Brother, my Protector, and my Best Friend felt like insurmountable, irreplaceable losses – but I had no one with whom I could share my pain. My religious friends would not understand, and my mother would be disappointed in my rejection of her God. With suicide not being an acceptable alternative, my only choice was to keep putting one foot in front of the other, One Day at a Time (a phrase well-known to those in 12-step recovery programs).

I was unaware that I was working my way through the "tasks of mourning" outlined by JW Worden (Worden, J. W. (2009). Grief Counseling and Grief Therapy: A Handbook for the Mental Health Practitioner, Fourth Edition, Springer, N.Y.).

According to Mr. Worden, the four main tasks of mourning include:

1. Accepting the reality of the loss.
2. Working through the pain of Grief.
3. Adjusting to a new environment without the deceased (in my case, my former beliefs).
4. Withdrawing emotional energy from the deceased (my former beliefs) and reinvesting it in a new relationship. In other words, not denying my religious past but allowing myself to explore and experience new thoughts, beliefs, and ways of being.

THE BOOKSTORE EPISODE

Eventually, I gave myself permission to research what other religions taught. I was afraid, at first, even just *thinking* such thoughts. I had been taught to fear the devil and beware of his wily traps and deception. I knew he could be a sneaky angel of light, and that I could be tricked. While I was starting to suspect that the God of Christianity did not exist, I was, by no means, rid of supernatural superstitions.

One day, my desire to know the truth overcame my fear, and I snuck across the street to *Ted's Used Books* while my daughters were in school.

At Ted's, occult books were not on shelves with the rest of the books. Instead, they were kept behind a dramatic red velvet curtain, beneath a hand-lettered sign labelled "Occult & Alternative Religions."

Holding my breath, I pulled that curtain aside and closed it behind me, waiting for a holy lightning bolt to strike me dead. Heart pounding, it took a few minutes for the book titles to stop swimming in front of my fearful eyes. Finally, I found a textbook comparing Christianity, Islam, Buddhism, and Confucianism. It seemed scholarly enough that I could defend my purchase if any Christians saw me with it. After asking the cashier to place my purchase in a brown paper bag – as if it were pornographic - I ran home and immediately hid my scholarly book in the safest place I could think of: My underwear drawer. God himself would not look there!

Little by little, in private, I read through that book - and went back for more. I didn't know it, but time was winding down on my marriage, as well as my faith. Though it would be a painful road, I was on the path to setting myself free.

I began visiting my little used book store regularly, no longer afraid of breaking Christian taboos or having church members find me with unacceptable books. Topics that interested me the most were about things formerly forbidden: Astrology, psychic phenomena, out-of-body experiences, chakras, and reincarnation. I wanted to learn all about Eastern religions and New Age philosophies.

While my husband and I still did not discuss the changes taking place in our marriage, it was undeniable that changes were taking place in me. Though I still struggled with the "What if I'm wrong?" fear, curiosity pulled me forward.

Recognizing that I no longer belonged with my former Christian community, I began constructing one that was *spiritual but not religious*.

I started playing the didgeridoo, taking my djembe to drum circles, meditating, attending yoga, and hanging out at the local "holistic wellness center," where I could also buy crystals and get Reiki sessions. I dove in deep and was delighted to find a welcoming, kind, and supportive community.

I especially loved attending sound healing sessions hosted by a woman I referred to as my spiritual teacher, where we would lie on the ground inside a local pyramid (at an organic winery). With candles lit and our eyes closed, she would wander between us playing her didgeridoo, singing bowls, wooden flutes, and other exotic-feeling instruments that whisked us away to the Land of Woo.

Shelves formerly reserved for Bibles, books on how to be a wife of noble character (according to Proverbs 31:10), and how to biblically discipline children were becoming weighted down instead by my singing bowls, Buddhas, and books to help align my chakras. For the first time in my life, I felt like I was hanging with the cool kids. I hadn't started engaging in critical thinking yet, so I didn't see that I was just swapping out one set of magical beliefs for another.

One weekend morning, I went for coffee with a coworker who was becoming a good friend. She inspired me as intelligent and independent, having recently left her husband and restarted her life as a single woman. I trusted my friend to speak earnestly with me and felt safe making what felt like a HUGE revelation to her: "Can I tell you something?" I asked. She nodded and leaned in close across the café table since I was nearly whispering. Gulping, I shared my innermost thoughts: *"I'm starting to doubt whether Adam and Eve were real people!"* Laughing, my friend patted my hand and assured me that she'd figured that out by age 7 – but she was glad I was catching up. Her confidence and reassurance made me smile.

With my own thoughts changing so drastically, I felt it was time for a frank discussion with my children. The girls were about 11 and 13 at the time, and like it or not, they had front-row seats to my messy deconversion. Now far less fearful that I was damning them to Hell by my apostasy, I decided it was time to bring up some of my changing beliefs with them.

When I told our youngest that I was reconsidering whether some of the Bible stories were actually true, she informed me that she never had been able to believe them herself. This was truly shocking to me, as I had done my best to indoctrinate her from birth. Her older sister declared that I seemed more relaxed since leaving religion which, again, came as a total shock to me. I had thought myself the picture of a gentle, merciful, and loving mother who happened to follow Jesus. While this was often true, my rigid worldview and insistence on following rules could also make me tyrannical if I feared their disobedience to scripture might make my children Hell-bound.

As fundamentalist Christianity loosened its grip, I could feel myself blooming after years of existing in a parched desert. Though mourning the significant and multiple losses of my belief system, identity, and community, I was free to explore anything and everything. I moved from a black-and-white, rigid worldview to a wide-open space bounded only by my curiosity and ethics — just to bounce back into grief unexpectedly. I felt like a steel ball in a cosmic pinball game. Who was I, if no longer a devout Christian, homeschooling, anti-feminist wife and mother?

Since we were both devout Christians when we met and married, it hadn't mattered that I'd been indoctrinated from birth while my husband had converted in his late teens. Now that I have a greater understanding of religious trauma syndrome, I appreciate the differences between those circumstances. My personality did not have the opportunity to develop apart from my parents' religious beliefs. My likes and dislikes were only permitted to develop within the confines of what was acceptable to

Jesus. This was true in matters that ranged from clothing and musical tastes to how to spend money and leisure time.

As a counsellor and coach working with my clients who are recovering from religious trauma and deconstructing their religious ideologies, one of the first exercises I assign them is that of values clarification. The goal is to start seeing themselves as separate from their parents, pastor, and former belief system. Previously, they likely prized obedience and humility as among their top values; now, they might instead place autonomy or curiosity at the top of their list.

Having such insight for myself in real time would have been helpful. Not having such insight set me up to run as far in the other direction as possible, determined to experience all I felt I'd been denied. I was immature, inexperienced, and vulnerable. The pendulum was picking up momentum with each pass, ensuring that my deconversion would be messy and painful for my family.

Being less prone to emotionally driven behavior and not having been indoctrinated from birth, my husband had a hard time fully understanding why my behavior associated with rejecting Christianity was so extreme.

HIGHER EDUCATION?

In my continued efforts to build my new identity while liberating myself from religious programming, I decided to secretly take an online course from a New Age diploma mill. I saw it as an opportunity to explore other beliefs while learning to guide myself and others in meditation and "psychic healing." While it appealed greatly to me, I didn't dare tell my husband what I was up to, not wanting a lecture on how I was wasting my money on things he did not believe.

To my delight, there were books and booklets to read through and assignments to complete as I became ever more acquainted with my spiritual-but-not-religious self. Additionally, after paying the required amount and handing in all assignments, I would finally get "letters" after my name, providing me a form of validation I yearned for after so many years as a mere wife and mother.

Over two full years (commence eyeball rolling now), my higher education unfolded thusly:

- First, I attained my Practitioner's Diploma from the *International Metaphysical Ministry University Seminary*, after which I could "engage in the treatment of physical and mental ailments and conditions through the use of spiritual mind treatment."

- Next came my ordination as a Metaphysical Minister through the same (highly reputable?) institution, so that I could apply to conduct weddings and other important spiritual occasions.

- Completing additional readings and assignments led to my "Bachelor" of Metaphysical Science.

- Undaunted, I pressed on to receive the highly coveted "Master" of Metaphysical Science, or M. MSc. through the (almost esteemed) *University of Metaphysics, Higher Education Division of the International Metaphysical Ministry, Inc.*

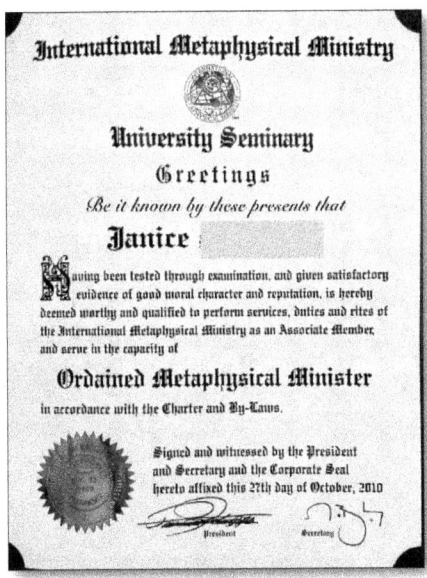

Being ordained as a Minister felt like a powerful *F-you* to the Christian Patriarchy

I took my practitioner role seriously, truly wanting to help my clients

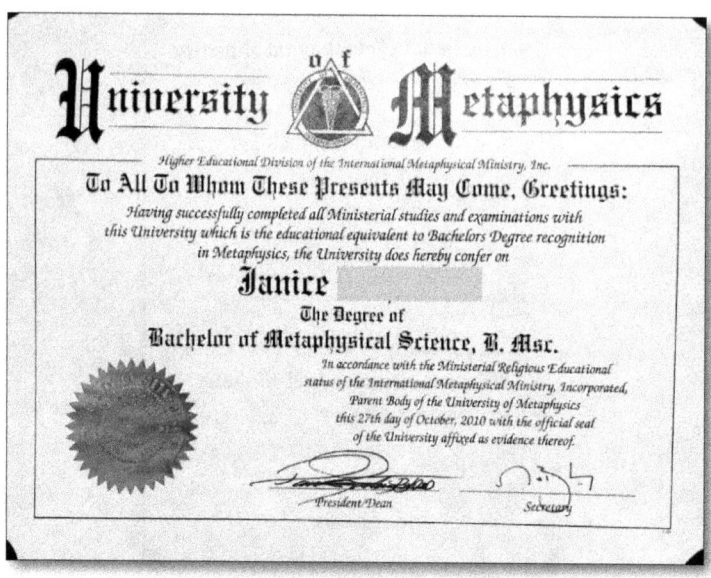

**Now, having achieved my *Bachelor*,
I believed I was really getting somewhere!**

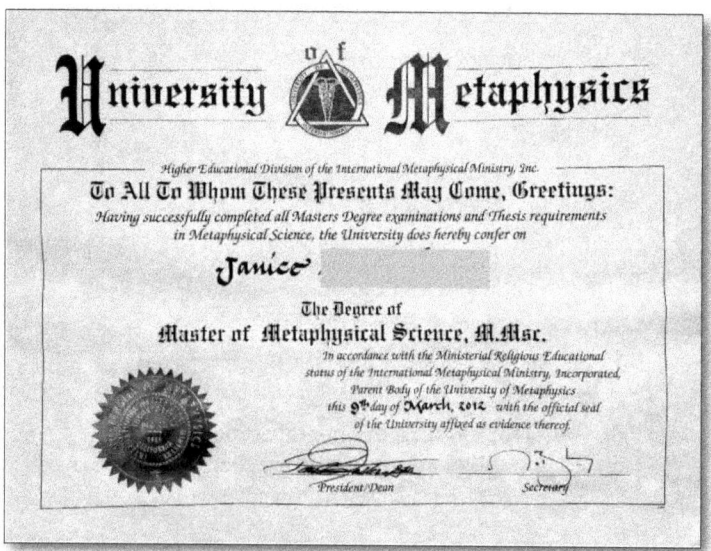

**TA-DA! What could feel more validating than being awarded
a *Master* of Metaphysical Science?**

These exciting points of validation were conferred upon me by the (not entirely) renowned *University of Metaphysics International*. I told myself that they were a legitimate organization because actress Della Reese (from the "Touched by an Angel" TV show) had received her doctorate through them. Also, the papers came with a shiny gold sticker, from the spiritual mecca of Los Angeles, CA.

However, even after framing my M. MSc., I couldn't quite bring myself to hang it where others might see it. The adage remains true: You can't fool yourself.

Though I wanted to return to a "real" university and complete the legitimate BA I had started before our marriage, our bankruptcy meant student loans would not be available to me. Additionally, my husband was still angry with me for his pastoral career failing and strongly discouraged me from pursuing higher education. He was stuck and, it seemed, felt that I should be, too.

About this time, our pastor/friend/landlord unexpectedly raised our rent by a huge amount, after assuring us that he would never do so. Angry and disappointed, we moved to another rental home and put both kids into public school. I felt deeply wounded by this man whom I had known since I was 14 years old. He and his wife knew of our bankruptcy, our significant marital pressures, and that our daughter's health was precarious – but they had no problem raising our rent by an exorbitant amount. This created an irreparable rift between us and added to my frustration around Christianity.

Putting our kids into public school was especially stressful for me regarding our youngest, who would be entering the zoo atmosphere of junior high while still learning to cope with her life-threatening illness. I was fearful of what bullies at that age might do. At this same time, our oldest was starting to act out as normal teens tend to do.

When her younger sister was diagnosed with a life-threatening illness, all of our spare energy and attention necessarily focused on our ill child. With our marriage barely holding together, our eldest daughter was often left on her own emotionally and physically. While we praised her for being independent, we failed to see her growing disconnection from our family.

My failure to provide our eldest with adequate nurturing and attention during that time still haunts me. As she began acting out, I was without any framework for parenting outside of being authoritarian, so it was a challenge. I lacked the time, energy, and now the religious impetus to encourage (formerly, to demand) obedience.

I am horrified by the abusive flavor of advice I received from Christian "parenting experts" when raising my children. My fear of raising a disobedient, sinful child ensured that I took discipline very seriously. NOTHING was more important than my children following the rules. I am sad that religious rigidity prevented me from simply enjoying my daughters' innate curiosity and normal efforts at expressing their unique personalities.

Not surprisingly, my first-born received the most parental scrutiny and harshest discipline. As she got older, in a typical Christian refusal to honor my child's boundaries, I read her diary.

Following further Christian advice, when I deemed my daughter's room untidy, I swept under her bed and dumped whatever I found onto her bedsheets.

Fundamentalism instilled a fear of my children rejecting Christianity that made me far stricter than my parents had been. I had placed unbearable pressure on my eldest child, essentially putting her into an impossible situation. She did not have the freedom to voice her opinion or get upset when she thought me unreasonable. I was re-creating the unhealthy parenting dynamic I'd experienced in my own family of origin when I'd been so disempowered by my dad. It's hard for me to share these failures publicly, but it's also important. I've expressed specific and sincere apologies since those days, but my words cannot undo the harm caused.

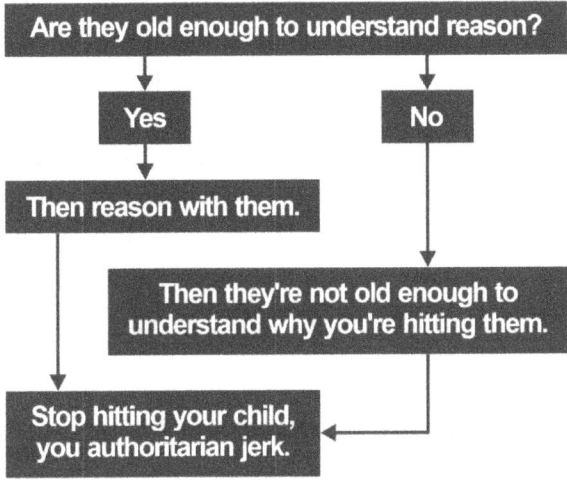

How I feel now about what I did then

The unanticipated move to another neighborhood, caused by our increased rent, added to our family strain. After our youngest daughter's diagnosis, I shifted from working at the hospital to doing medical transcription from home. Delighted with my spiritual growth and my new metaphysical designations, I wanted to continue moving in that direction. After a weekend course in relaxation massage at our local college, *Soul Pilgrim Holistic Services* was open for business in our newly rented home. I even started a blog chronicling my divorce from religion, which still exists online at Soul Pilgrims Welcome (*see Chapter 7 Resources*).

The combination of medical transcription and the personal interaction with massage clients suited me well. I decorated my massage room with an Eastern flare and loved the feeling of helping people, some of whom sought my help with developing personal meditation routines. However, my marriage continued to fracture.

We still avoided discussing my changing beliefs. My husband continued to blame me for the loss of his church leadership dream, and I carried the weight of that judgment. My refusal to remain obedient or submissive any longer created added discomfort, but I was determined to chart my own course. I aimed for the success that had eluded him, though I chafed at the feeling of competition further dividing us.

When my husband's obsession with the video game waned, he asked if I would consider starting a classic rock band with him playing '70s and '80s music. His rhythmic challenges made it hard, but it was also fun. Our band served the additional purpose of temporarily diverting attention from the fact that we were seriously mismatched.

CHAPTER 7 LINKS & RESOURCES

CHAPTER EIGHT

GOODBYE, PURITY CULTURE!

One inescapable difference between my husband and me was how we expressed our love to each other. I thrived on words of affirmation, while he found them unnecessary and embarrassing. I recall specifically telling him that I *needed* to hear him say that he thought I was beautiful - and his factual reply that doing so would be disingenuous. In short, I felt like a piece of furniture.

The Uncovering

I continued liberating myself from religious judgment and loved the attention of being on stage. During this time I started to face another aspect of my selfhood that had not previously been permitted to surface: My attraction to women. When I tentatively brought this up with my husband, I was surprised by his lack of surprise.

While his failure to read the emotions of others was legendary, after a decade and a half together it seemed that he could at least read between my lines in the bedroom.

I felt like the pressure was landing solidly on my shoulders to hold our marriage together and stated that I didn't think I could hang on - unless we moved to an open-marriage model. That idea held no appeal for him, but he *did* concede to my pursuing discreet relationships with other women. His compassionate willingness to allow me this freedom was a lifeline. I was tired of living with Mr. Spock and needed to connect, emotionally and intimately, with others. In a flash, I set up my dating profile.

The first time I remember feeling attracted to a woman was as an adolescent watching the TV show WKRP in Cincinnati in the 1970s. My brothers and father were enamored of actress Loni Anderson, but I found myself crushing on Jan Smithers, who played journalist Bailey Quarters. During that era, I also happened upon an iconic poster of model and actress Farrah Fawcett in her red bathing suit which made my heart skip a beat. It seemed odd that women could evoke the same sort of "crush" reaction I had towards some of the boys at my school, but I didn't think much more about it. When I entered my extremely puritanical phase in junior high, I determined to quash my attraction to women, understanding such desires to be sinful according to the Bible.

With my husband generously agreeing to look the other way and ignore my activities, I began interacting with women online who were either lesbians, bisexual, or just curious. I wasn't interested in being part of a threesome, as that felt like cheating – which let out the majority of respondents to my profile.

Enjoying the company of women felt both natural and exciting. I met up with a younger woman in my town who was a total stranger to me. A university student, she was as curious as me and wanted to find out what it would be like to be sexually intimate with another female. We chatted several times online and then plucked up all of our courage to meet in a public park, both terrified that the other had a dangerous male lover hiding nearby. Once we felt safe enough, we decided to head over to her place and see what happened.

While we both felt awkward and clumsy, it was still enjoyable and very steamy. I realized, without any doubt, that I am bisexual. While the young woman was very attractive, I was looking for a partner closer to my stage in life.

Not long after, I met a woman closer to my age but farther from my home. April and I enjoyed a fairly steady long-distance relationship which felt safer, as there was less chance of my regular life being interrupted with her living a few hours away. We would meet each other on long weekends a few times per year, both of our husbands knowing about the arrangement.

Speaking of cultural appropriation, please excuse my dreadnots and didgeridonts

April was tall and slender with long blonde and grey dreadlocks that created a stir wherever she went. I was so taken with how they looked, and the freedom she embodied, that I decided to grow dreadlocks myself, not the least bit thoughtful of potential cultural appropriation.

To me, dreadlocks symbolized my liberation from an uptight religious sheep to a free-thinking, I'll-try-anything-once adult. With my daughters' help, my hair was separated and twisted into baby dreads.

A true hippie, April had none of the religious baggage I sought to shed. She and her husband hosted drumming circles and smoked weed in their backyard, which felt edgy and dangerous and heightened my attraction to her. She loved nature and crystals and drove a Jeep.

April had a lightheartedness that made her very attractive to me. With both of us keen on New Age woo, she encouraged me to explore spirituality apart from religion, delving more deeply into tarot cards and chakra alignment.

Threading beads onto my dreads felt extra rebellious

She preferred homeopathy to pharmaceuticals and always smelled of incense. I have many fond memories of our times together and still treasure a pair of earrings she gave me on one of our first nights together.

LIFE IN A PRESSURE COOKER

Wanting to live in a better neighborhood, our family moved again within my hometown. Since it was a more expensive neighborhood, I felt pressured to take a full-time office job that offered medical and dental benefits. I accepted a position at a local business college as a medical transcription instructor and recognized almost immediately that it was a *huge* mistake.

The college was poorly run and the pressure was intense. When I told my husband that I had made a mistake and wanted to go back to my previous work arrangement and just work more hours from home, he balked. His resentment and anger came out full force as he hissed "Good! Now YOU can know what it's like to be stuck in a job you hate!"

I was stunned. I had fully supported him in changing out of a profession he hated (construction) into one that he had wanted (theology). Then, after pastoring failed, I continued encouraging him to consider other professions because he was so miserable doing construction. Unfortunately, declaring bankruptcy had made it impossible for him to take out another student loan, leaving him feeling more stuck than ever.

Intensely discouraged and deeply frustrated, I continued with my job at the career college, dreading it every day. Our marriage hung by a thread as I now knew the full level of his resentment towards me. By now, I was circling the drain of depression over my emotionally unsustainable situation. Something had to give – and it was the last something I ever would have suspected.

Our classic rock band was gaining notoriety and the kids seemed fairly settled. I continued exploring alternative spiritualities and developed some supportive friendships along the way, but it was not enough. Feeling stuck in a job I hated was too much. My husband threatened to move us back to the prairies if I quit my job - a threat I could not tolerate. It was impossible to reason with him and it felt like we had reached a serious stalemate.

A stranger had heard about my Soul Pilgrim business, and I received a request to attend an "alternative spirituality" festival a couple of hours away. I was encouraged to bring my massage chair and was asked to offer the opening prayer in a sort of New Age, non-threatening, Jesus-is-my-guru kind of way.

Initially, I was excited, but the night before I was to go I was having very strong second thoughts. I cried and told my husband I just didn't want to go. I was not used to going anywhere by myself, I didn't know how to get to the location, and I wouldn't know anyone there. My anxiety ran deeper than just those reasons, however. Neither my husband nor I knew that attending the festival would put the final nail into our coffin. He encouraged me to go since I could potentially make money off the massages.

FALL FROM GRACE

Upon arriving at the festival, I could see it was chaotic and poorly prepared. No one seemed to know where I was supposed to stay. Since I was told I would be staying in a building with other "leaders," I didn't bring a tent. Eventually, I connected with someone who took me to a house on the property. I was to share an upstairs room with a few other strangers who had helped put the event together.

Outside, I set up my massage chair beneath a tent-like structure at the festival and started to feel more relaxed. As requested, I opened the festival with a generic, spiritual-but-not-religious prayer and enjoyed feeling, once again, like I was with the cool kids. I was older than most of the attendees, but they seemed to accept me and kept me busy at the massage chair. I would have been happy to try psychedelics, had they been offered, but only alcohol was on the menu. Eventually, I made my way back to my room for the night, giddy with feelings of success and acceptance.

Only one other person ever showed up in the room that had been set aside for four of us. He introduced himself as Keith (not his real name) and stated that he needed the bed due to a back issue. I told him I was fine on the floor. This was the only time I had been in a bedroom with another man since getting married. We talked quite a bit, and I could sense that he was attracted to me. Eventually, he invited me off the floor, and I accepted with not-too-surprising results.

My feelings were at once elation and guilt. For the first time in over a decade, a man expressed desire for me. It had been a long time since I didn't just feel like a piece of furniture. As cliché as it sounds, I felt alive for the first time in many years. We exchanged email addresses though thought it unlikely we would meet again, as he lived in a different town.

When I returned to work on Monday, my office mate asked "What happened? You're glowing!" and I spilled the beans to her. Like so many others, I wanted to have my cake and eat it too. I justified my actions to myself by saying that my kids and husband needed me in their lives for stability - but that I also needed (deserved, even) to feel wanted, cherished, and alive.

It didn't take long before my husband figured something was different about me. Foolishly, I had emailed Keith about our forbidden time together. As this was my first attempt at deceiving my husband, I had no idea how to cover my tracks. While I was at work, he found the deleted emails from Keith, and the jig was up.

Never have I felt such shame. I was not just upset that my betrayal had been discovered; I was truly horrified by my actions. For the first time in my life, I came face-to-face with the fact that I was just like any other human. I could no longer pride myself on living a life that was above reproach. My self-righteousness and pretense disintegrated.

Fifteen years of faithful marriage, trying my best to be a good wife and partner, sincerely behaving as a devoted mother – all of these vaporized and no longer counted for anything. Aware of what I could lose, I kneeled before my husband in contrition, sobbing uncontrollably. I sincerely apologized and promised it would never happen again, but that was not enough. Years of frustration and disappointment about his life and our marriage boiled over.

Gripped with understandable rage, he determined to tell our daughters what I had done. I begged him not to burden them in this way, but he was deaf to my pleas. He called them both upstairs and told them they would not be going to school that day because he had something important to tell them: Their mother was having an affair. Of course, they were dumbfounded.

I insisted that it had *not* been an ongoing affair; that it was one night that I deeply regretted. While this felt like an important detail to me at the time, the fact that I had exchanged emails with Keith left the possibility open for further infidelity.

My youngest daughter opened her mouth and howled an inhuman sound. Grief, anger, fear, disappointment, and whatever other emotions she was feeling poured out in that agonizing scream.

I was overcome with rage at their father for subjecting them to this pain and was steeped in shame and self-recrimination. What could I do but apologize to all of them, repeatedly? I did not even beg their forgiveness, for I did not feel I deserved it. I had betrayed the very people I loved the most, and nothing could undo my thoughtless actions. Many years later, tears still sting my eyes as I share this painful truth here.

To my utter surprise, both of my daughters approached me over the following days and offered their forgiveness for my betrayal. Both girls stated that they knew about my frustration of life with their father, because they experienced it, too (look up "Cassandra Syndrome" for more on this).

Eventually, my husband agreed not to proceed directly with divorce. Instead, he would track my phone everywhere and check on me whenever I wasn't home. I agreed, to try and salvage the marriage and mitigate the pain for our daughters. This was not sustainable, however, as it just felt like we were both in jail. After a few weeks, I knew neither of us would be happy with this arrangement, and moved into a different bedroom in our home.

I once again reached out to my family physician, letting her know what was going on. I started antidepressants, determined to remain living in the same house with my daughters and their dad for as long as possible. My doctor suggested that the strain of my new job was the likely catalyst and straw that finally broke the camel's back. She wondered whether my infidelity was rooted in my ultimate desire to be free from a difficult marriage, recognizing it as the one act from which no recovery was possible. Deeply saddened, I recognized the truth of her words.

We settled into a somewhat uneasy peace. We were not angry. There was no yelling or fighting, just tremendous sorrow and grief. I still had to keep working at the job I hated, but now I felt even more trapped. Without a financial partner, how could I quit and aim for something better? I doubted that I would ever be able to take care of myself financially.

Eventually, my husband also developed an online dating profile. Far from being jealous, I offered to check it over for him before publishing. While we were headed for divorce, we remained kind to each other. Neither of us wanted the other to hurt any more than we already were.

It's been said that dating after divorce is like high school, only with debt and stretch marks. This is not far wrong. After being married for nearly two decades, it felt weird to publicly be "back on the market." I expanded my former dating profile (which had been for dating only other women) to include a profile also open to men.

Coming from a conservative background, however, meant that I was still somewhat naïve when it came to dating. Receiving unsolicited dick pics was shocking and unwelcome, adding to the trauma of all I was going through. Even when I thought a person had partnership potential, being ghosted after an enjoyable date made me realize that I had just been used to gratify a man's desire. It was a huge learning curve.

Those of us who venture onto the dating scene after decades in a marriage, especially during a time of personal religious deconstruction, are extremely vulnerable. We have very little real-world experience and lag behind our secular peers in many ways. I presented myself honestly and expected others to do the same, which was often not the case. I often felt pressured into physical intimacy before I was ready. In some cases, this was assault, but it didn't register to me as such because the concept of "consent" was not one I had explored as a religious woman.

This vulnerability can also be significant for those who grew up under toxic purity culture indoctrination and who remained single and chaste. In my counselling practice, I work with former fundamentalists who have reached mid-to-late life with no experience dating or relating romantically to others because they were "saving themselves" for a godly spouse.

For more on this, explore videos from my Shameless Sexuality: Life After Purity Culture conference on the Divorcing Religion YouTube channel. See Chapter 8 Resources for the link.

After about a year of living with my husband while separated, I moved into a small apartment on my own. Thanks to a dating app I was dating one man consistently, and a year later I moved into his high-end condo. About 5 years younger than me, "Luke" (not his real name) was the opposite of my husband in many ways. He owned a luxury travel company and exposed me to a lifestyle that I had never imagined possible, living downtown and traveling to exotic destinations.

My youngest daughter was still in high school, and she stayed with us once a week. She and Luke shared many interests, and she grew to love him as an additional father figure. At the time, I failed to see that some of their shared interests were immature for an adult male.

To my delight, my parents and extended family—and even my soon-to-be ex-husband—would come over for family dinners on birthdays and holidays. While my friends and my mother were somewhat skeptical of Luke's intentions, I was thrilled to be living the high life, in more ways than one.

No longer bound by the moral constraints of religion, I determined to give myself total freedom to explore (during the times my daughter was not present). Luke got a kick out of seeing me have new experiences and told me that *nothing was off-limits* and that he would foot the bill. I tried many mind-altering substances and consumed more alcohol than in all of my previous years combined.

It was the adolescence I never had. One experience stands out to this day: My first time trying MDMA (or "Molly," as it is sometimes known). I had no idea what to expect, other than people had said it made them feel very happy. I was in the bathroom in my bikini before we went for a dip in the hot tub. I looked in the mirror – and for the very first time in my entire life, I felt overwhelmed with LOVE for myself. Luke heard me sobbing and ran in to see what was wrong. I pointed to my reflection in the mirror and sobbed "Look at me! I am *so fucking beautiful!*"

While I went on to do a lot more tripping (some pleasant, others not so much), that experience remains a precious highlight.

In addition to giving myself the freedom to try whatever substances I desired, I was also willing to explore sex with other partners—much to Luke's delight. While he said he loved me, he also stated that he did not want to be "hemmed in;" thus, our relationship took on a somewhat open flavor. This would not have been my first choice, but I feared losing him if I objected. I now had a vague sense of the pressure my husband must have felt when I demanded we move to an open marriage.

While not wanting to appear prudish, I did set out some ground rules for Luke:

- He could fool around with other women when he was out of town for business, provided he was careful and did not bring me back any type of STI.

- Locally, we could enjoy being with other people sexually *as a couple, only*. I did not want him seeking out private liaisons in our town.

- Finally, I told him that I did not want him to build emotional bonds with other women; it was to be sex, only.

These seemed like reasonable requests to me, and he agreed. I congratulated myself on my continued growth and liberation.

As with the drinking and drug experimentation, liberated sexuality felt very much like another adolescence. After nearly 20 years with the same sexual partner, I was happy to open myself to these new experiences. We met other couples online and had them over, deciding whether or not we wanted to take things any further. It felt amazing to be so free and I was not encumbered by any sense of guilt or shame. I was curious and eager to explore, denying myself nothing.

Luke's parties were legendary, whether large or small. He was proud to provide party favors (booze and drugs) for all in attendance. Once I was feeling a good buzz, I would head outside to enjoy the quiet stillness of our 7th floor balcony while the party continued indoors. Under a cozy blanket on our loveseat, I stared up at the stars, psilocybin creating intensely colorful visual hallucinations and a feeling of deep connection to the universe. Familiar waves of spiritual ecstasy washed over me, similar to what I had experienced in my old church days, when all the Believers were singing praises to God and speaking in tongues.

The hedonistic life I lived with Luke was vastly different from my confined life as a Christian wife and mother—except for when my daughter was over. During those times, Party Girl was banished, and Mom was on duty.

BACK TO SCHOOL

Living with Luke meant that I could afford to go back to school. I left the business college job I'd hated so much and returned to working part-time at the hospital so that I could do my studies while at home. I enrolled at a college that specializes in professional counsellor training and began simultaneously looking forward to my new career while looking back at my life experiences.

For the first time, I began learning about the impacts of trauma and recognizing some of my own trauma responses. I started unpacking my childhood with a father who showed narcissistic tendencies and who was also a religious fundamentalist – but I was not ready to connect all the dots just yet. I knew that loud noises and yelling impacted me viscerally thanks to complex PTSD from years of his volatility and raging tantrums, but I didn't yet understand the role that religion played in my trauma.

During my counsellor training, I was exposed to information about *the Sixties Scoop* in Canada for the first time. I was sickened to learn the truth about Indian Residential Schooling and the cultural genocide perpetrated against Indigenous people in my own country, starting with the Indian Act of 1876. The Canadian government and the Catholic

Church (along with Anglican, United, Presbyterian, and other Christian churches) were all guilty.

Now concerned that my white, Evangelical family had inadvertently participated in the cultural genocide of First Nations people by fostering my sister, I began exploring our somewhat strained relationship. Cautiously, I reached out to her. I was finally starting to grasp what it may have been like to be taken away from her own family and forced to live with non-indigenous religious strangers.

My sister was extremely gracious in accepting my apology for having been thoroughly ignorant about Canada's history and how it painfully impacted her own life. We remain in contact today and enjoy a kind and supportive relationship.

I also began learning about NPD, or narcissistic personality disorder. Narcissism is generally viewed on a spectrum, and I was fascinated to recognize aspects of this trait in partners and family members, as well as in myself. It also made sense to me that leaders of cults and high-demand groups (including religious ones) are often narcissistic.

Like many who grew up in challenging homes, my draw to a career in the field of mental health was almost impossible to resist. I was a natural when it came to listening and empathy and knew that I would truly love my work. After graduating, I hung my shingle and saw my clientele grow quickly by word of mouth. I felt pride in seeing clients in the cozy, professional office I'd set up in our luxury condo. While Christianity was in my rearview mirror, I was happily ensconced in my spiritual-but-not-religious New Age community.

Ironically, the man I selected as my counselling supervisor (a requirement for my professional designation) was a devout Christian. I chose him because he was a respected local grief counsellor with many years of experience. I felt that I could learn much from him, though I was uncomfortable any time he brought up religion. Since he asked me point blank if I had accepted Jesus as my personal savior, I thought he might have been unwilling to take me on as his supervisee if he knew I no longer believed - so I feigned agreement and kept my views to myself. I now recognize his question as unprofessional and unacceptable, even though he cared earnestly about me and his clients.

Missing the sense of community from my religious days, I decided to start my own spiritual community. I advertised the first meeting of the Soul Sisters on Facebook and was delighted when about 10 women showed up. We met monthly in Luke's luxury condo, and I felt happy and proud of the life I was building. With these women, I discussed psychic phenomena, reincarnation, and all things supernatural. I loved the freedom to explore with them what was formerly forbidden to me and felt at home in a position of leadership.

While I enjoyed my interactions with these women, it eventually became clear that New Age beliefs were just as unfounded as my former supernatural Christian ones. This became apparent when several Soul Sisters urged me to attend an expensive evening with a woman who claimed to channel a Being from the spirit realm. Interestingly, while this Being supposedly existed "beyond the realms of time and space," it was not beyond charging exorbitant fees for tickets to view the channeling episodes. Disappointed that my friends believed such nonsense, my time in the New Age community came to an end. Though I didn't recognize it yet, I was taking my first steps along the road to critical thinking.

CHAPTER 8 LINKS & RESOURCES

CHAPTER NINE

ALL THAT GLITTERS

Eventually, I grew tired of the prolonged adolescence that epitomized life with Luke. Partying every weekend was taking a toll on my body, and I didn't feel that the questionable activities in our private life fit in with my new career. I was growing up. My curiosity had been satiated, and I wanted a more traditional type of relationship with Luke, minus all the party favors.

Accordingly, I had finally taken Luke up on his offer "to make an honest man" of him by accepting his suggestion that we get married. We chose a ring to be designed for me, and he was excited to invite friends on a luxury cruise to witness our engagement. But when I expressed to him that I wanted to pull back from the party lifestyle we had been living for the past few years, he balked at the suggestion.

He seemed distant after that discussion when we took a trip together, but I wrote it off as work stress. I was disappointed when he refused to accompany me to a memorial service for my aunt and uncle just a few hours away, but I didn't press the matter. On my return, I noted that he was less interested in sex, which was unusual.

During yet another party at our place, one of Luke's edgier friends (a criminal-turned-tattoo-artist) approached me and remarked on the open nature of our relationship. Having not discussed this previously with him, I found the conversation somewhat disconcerting and wondered what he had heard or seen.

The next night, when we were alone, Luke blurted out "I can't do this anymore." I assumed he felt pressure around our coming engagement, so I told him it wasn't necessary; I was happy to continue in our committed relationship without marriage. What he was referring to, however, was cheating on me.

I didn't know that Luke had been actively breaking the generous relationship "rules" we had agreed on at the start of our cohabitation. To my heartbreaking surprise, he had thrown a party and was openly affectionate with another woman while I was away at my relatives' memorial service. When people inquired, he told them that I knew all about it and was supportive; hence, the discussion with his tattoo artist friend.

When I pressed Luke about why he was ending our relationship, he stated that he just did not love me anymore. When I asked if he was seeing someone else, he emphatically lied, "No! I could never do that to you." In an instant, my world went into a tailspin of grief unlike any I had known.

The sudden and complete loss of our relationship hit me harder than the loss of both my faith and my marriage, as I had been extremely happy with Luke and loved the life that I thought we were building together. I expected that we had hit a speed bump rather than the end of the road, but I was wrong. Believing him when he denied there being anyone else, I felt helpless to change the situation. He was not willing to attend couple's therapy.

I felt confused, heartbroken, and sick to my stomach. Sleep was a welcome relief – until I woke up in our bed to remember that my life had fallen apart and plunged back into hysterical sobbing. Within 24 hours, Luke had gone from saying "I love you" to being stone silent. Nothing I said could move him; he was resolute that our life together was finished and insisted that I move out as quickly as possible.

I was emotionally destitute and would now be financially destitute, as well. He agreed to pay me a pittance of support for 12 months as I tried to get on my feet, but I no longer had an office in which to see clients (this was before the days of on-line therapy).

One evening, my ex-husband and I ran into each other. I told him he had every right to enjoy my heartache, as I was now reaping the cheating behavior I had sown at the end of our marriage. He shook his head sadly and told me he was only sorry to see my suffering.

A genuine friendship had been able to grow between us over the intervening years we'd been apart. I was no longer frustrated by my former spouse's lack of emotional interaction, and he no longer felt stuck in a relationship with a woman it felt impossible to please. We could finally support one another as friends. We still do today.

Still in disbelief over my sudden and unwelcome change in circumstance, I moved into a grimy illegal basement suite on the edge of town. Dirty and unfinished, it was all I could afford on my own. The kitchen did not meet safety codes, so I had to wear rubber gloves and stand on a rubber mat to try and ground myself for unplugging the stove to plug in the clothes dryer. More than once, I received a nasty electric shock. The landlord was handsome but a bad boy, right down to riding a Harley Davidson. He lived upstairs and did not care about codes of any kind. We both knew low vacancy rates meant others would happily move in if I moved out.

I returned to working full-time at the hospital, frequently typing through silent tears. Walking back to my car alone at the end of my shifts, I often sobbed hysterically. This was a very dark time for me emotionally. I didn't see how I could return to my counselling practice without having a space in which to see clients.

A couple of months after the breakup, I started receiving Facebook messages from people telling me how sorry they were. I didn't understand what they were talking about until a friend called from out of town and told me to look at Luke's Facebook profile. He had taken a woman who resembled me, though a much younger version, on our "engagement" cruise and was posting multiple photos of how happy they were together. To my dismay, his family members posted extremely supportive comments.

I recognized the other woman immediately, as he had invited her to some gatherings at our home previously. Once again, I was emotionally gutted by the man my daughter and I had loved. It felt like one minute I was sitting at my beautiful dining room table with him, enjoying our life together; then the roof was lifted off, Monty Python style, and I was plucked up and set outside, staring in through the picture window at another woman who was now sitting in my spot. My life had changed without my consent and I was powerless to do anything about it. Rage, depression, and disbelief became my companions.

Desperate to find something good about my new living situation, I explored my rural neighborhood, above the city and filled with orchards. I discovered podcasts and started listening to them during my daily walks. One huge, panoramic viewpoint on my walk opened the valley breathtakingly before me. My practice became, at that point on my walk, to stand firmly, open my arms wide, and yell, "I release you! I release you!" in an attempt to expunge Luke from my heart, not wanting to be saddled with despair and bitterness for the rest of my life.

LEVI

Levi (not his real name), the bad boy owner of my grimy basement suite, lived upstairs. He was rugged and handsome, about 12 years younger than me. While he was hardly my type, I was extremely vulnerable in my grief. Within a few months of my living there, he expressed interest beyond the typical landlord-tenant relationship. Having been so publicly rejected for a younger woman, it felt powerful that a much younger man —one more athletically fit than Luke - found me attractive.

Levi and I had nothing in common, and he was swimming in murky legal water by initiating a sexual relationship with his tenant due to the power differential between us. I was fragile and raw, still very much in the depths of my grief, feeling like I did after getting dumped by my first serious boyfriend. Desperate to prove that I was still desirable, I followed the age-old advice, for good or ill: The quickest way to get over someone is to get under someone else.

The sex sizzled, but his proclivity for booze and party favors (especially cocaine) felt too familiar. Soon, I had to admit the truth that my young biker landlord was not long-term partner material. I was single once more.

Eventually, my daily walking, furious poetry writing, and prolific crying opened up emotional space so that I felt I could breathe again. I began to explore my co-dependent ways and vowed to choose more wisely in the future. Unfortunately, my good intentions and partial insights were not enough to protect me.

After about half a year, I was feeling more like myself again. I was working nearly full-time and not going under financially. Grief had knocked a pile of weight off, and I liked what I saw in the mirror. Men and women were expressing interest in dating me, and I was once again feeling empowered. My youngest daughter moved in with me, and after a few more months I began dating a fellow who seemed significantly more mature than Luke and Levi. He was smart and charming, and I proceeded with caution... or so I thought.

STILL MISSING RED FLAGS

James (not his real name) asked to move in with us more quickly than I felt comfortable with, as he had "lost his job" in a neighboring community and had no reason to remain there. We'd been dating for a few months, and I was falling in love with him, so I agreed to let him move in. A couple of years my senior, he seemed mature and thoughtful, and I was happy. Having helped update his resume, I saw that his work positions had been upper management on several large projects.

The only red flag was that he would never make or take phone calls in my presence from his family back in Toronto. *Reminder to self: Red flags just look like normal flags when one is wearing rose-colored glasses!* James assured me that he had been separated for many years from his wife and that they were in no way together anymore. He stated that she often provoked him to anger and he did not want me to hear him yelling, so he chose to speak with her away from me.

Still slightly leery, I insisted that James begin divorce proceedings once we were living together, as I did not want our relationship to be his dirty secret. He agreed and assured me that he would contact his lawyer to get things started. In the meantime, he asked me to understand his need to return to Toronto every couple of months to visit his two grown children and one pre-adolescent child. This seemed reasonable, and I tried to push my concerns under the metaphorical rug.

I believed that James was trustworthy because he was a follower of Reform Judaism, which he appeared to practice intermittently but spoke about fairly often. Occasionally, he asked me to attend his local synagogue. While it felt uncomfortable when they read from the Talmud (or Old Testament), it was nice to be welcomed into a community again. James assured me that they did not believe in a literal God or Hell or even Heaven; at least, not the way Christians do.

INTRODUCTION TO RELIGIOUS TRAUMA SYNDROME

During this time, I finally discovered that I was not alone in the pain I'd suffered from growing up deeply religious. After years of searching the internet for evidence that others were living healthy, happy lives post-religion, I saw a news clip featuring psychologist and author Dr. Marlene Winell.

In addition to her book *Leaving the Fold: A guide for former fundamentalists and others leaving their religion* (1993, New Harbinger Publications and 2007, Apocryphal Press), Dr. Winell is also the founder and director of the organization Journey Free: Recovery from Harmful Religion, which has information and services for individuals and groups.

The CNN interview with Dr. Winell followed a deadly shooting committed by a young man who blamed his Christian fundamentalist upbringing for the emotional pain that brought about his murderous rampage. During the interview, Dr. Winell shared her expertise about religious trauma. *See Chapter 9 Resources for a link to Dr. Winell's video interview and Journey Free.*

Dr. Winell coined the phrase "religious trauma syndrome," or RTS for short. She developed this term for a collection of symptoms often suffered by those who have spent time in high-control religions, experiencing loss both during their association with the high-control group and then experiencing additional loss upon leaving the group.

After finding Dr. Winell on the internet, I reached out to her and she invited me to attend one of her retreats in San Francisco for people recovering from RTS. I didn't know it then, but attending her retreat would be a turning point in my life and career. I felt terrified getting on the plane by myself, not knowing anyone else who would be there. What if this was just another religious cult? What if they kidnapped me and I was never heard from again? It took all my courage to go – and it was one of the best choices I've ever made.

Dr. Winell's retreat was my first time engaging with others who had been as devoted to their previous faith and had likewise walked away from their religions. While our religious backgrounds varied and our losses were not identical, we could each relate to the feelings that accompanied those losses. I was receiving validation and support for the first time since starting my divorce from religion.

Dr. Winell's book was a tremendous help to me, and I continue to recommend it to RTS survivors and therapists alike.

I returned to my basement suite, now shared with my daughter and James, and started to feel more positive about my situation. I was not yet a full atheist, but I was comfortable referring to myself as agnostic.

One memory stands out from around this time, as I was starting to understand the depth of my religious trauma. James and I were watching an episode of Star Trek: The Next Generation that had a storyline that revolved around evolution (Star Trek: The Next Generation: Season 7, Episode 19). James made a snide remark about how anyone could fail to accept evolution in our modern age, which utterly surprised me.

"But you're *Jewish!*" I exclaimed. "How can you BELIEVE in evolution?" He was quiet for a moment and then said he had no problem reconciling science with his version of Reform Judaism. When he gently asked me what I believed, I broke down in tears because I truly did not know anymore.

I wanted to believe in logic and reason and science, but for some reason accepting evolution presented a major hurdle for me. It was then that

James asked exactly how long I'd been out of religion, and I told him it had only been a few years. I had a long way to go on my journey. I knew who I wasn't, but I hadn't yet discovered who I was.

Shortly after this event, someone I barely knew gifted me with a free ticket to attend a local conference about learning to share our personal stories. At the crowning event of the weekend-long workshop each participant took center stage for about 10 minutes to tell their own story. In what became a pivotal life event, I decided to share the story of my religious deconversion, never having done so in public.

The night before, I rehearsed my *extimony* (the opposite of a religious testimony) for a couple of hours, wanting to share it without looking at my notes as best I could. The next afternoon, my sharing time came. I was cold and clammy as I looked out at the dozen or so people in the room, unsure how they would respond. Knowing that some religious people reject the possibility that their beliefs could traumatize anyone, I feared that some attendees might be offended and create an ugly scene.

When everyone was quiet, I told them of going from being absolutely certain of my faith and identity to losing it all, and how I had to summon every ounce of courage available to build a new life based on critical thinking and evidence rather than fiction and feelings.

You could have heard a pin drop. At times, I fought tears as I recounted my loss and anguish. When my time was up, everyone erupted in cheers. I didn't know it, but that first time sharing publicly was a major step along my journey. I remain grateful to Diane Currie Sam for that first opportunity to share my extimony and then for helping me to develop my story for presentation. *See Chapter 9 Resources for more information.*

Buoyed by the success of sharing my story in a small group, I applied next to speak at a women's event in my town which had about twice as many attendees as the workshop.

Surprisingly, my mother asked to attend the women's event so that she could gain insight into this part of my life. All she knew was that I was no longer religious. Though it felt slightly uncomfortable, I picked her up and brought her along. Regardless of whatever my mother thought or felt while I shared my experiences, she beamed at me and clapped heartily at the end. Happily, my story met with similar approval in this slightly larger venue. Each time I told my story, my confidence grew.

Eventually, James, I, and my youngest daughter moved out of Levi's basement suite into the top floor of a house where my eldest daughter was renting the basement with her partner. It felt perfect having both my girls under the same roof again, and things continued relatively smoothly with James. Every couple of months he left to visit his daughters in Toronto, and he assured me that they knew about me and that his divorce was well underway.

DIVORCING RELIGION WORKSHOP

In 2018, I decided to create a workshop for others exiting fundamentalist religions. I used my own research on cults, how beliefs are formed, my personal experience, and my education and training as a therapist. After several months, the *Divorcing Religion Workshop* was ready to share with the world. I began reaching out to podcasters in the atheist realm and expanding my social media presence, to spread the word about my workshop and develop the Divorcing Religion brand.

I happily invited others I'd met, through Dr. Winell and on podcasts, to participate in my first workshop for free, valuing their honest feedback about my course. Oddly, James asked if he could pretend to be recovering from religious trauma in order to attend the online workshop with others. I told him that would be utterly inappropriate, so he let the matter drop. For my part, it was another ignored red flag about James.

Once I had participants lined up, we met online each Sunday morning for 7 weeks to go through the Divorcing Religion Workshop. Participants came from varied backgrounds including Evangelical, Catholic, and Seventh Day Adventist.

I was especially happy when Paul, an older man I'd met through Dr. Winell's online support group, indicated that he would like to participate in the first round of my workshop. I had found him to be wise, kind, and thoughtful, and I suspected that he would have some helpful suggestions. Our friendship was cemented during the workshop and I knew he was someone I wanted to keep in my life.

Wanting to share my workshop with others, I began searching online for podcasts geared toward those recovering from religious trauma. One of the first groups I reached out to was Recovering from Religion, or RfR, an organization founded by psychologist and author Dr. Darrel Ray, a pioneer in the field of religious trauma recovery. RfR is now a global organization offering resources and support groups, in-person and online, around the world for those recovering from all religions. *See Chapter 9 Resources for more on RfR.*

After the success of my workshop and interacting with others who could relate to my faith loss, I felt more comfortable sharing my story of religious deconversion in public. I enjoyed being a regular guest on religious-trauma-related podcasts. When I saw an ad promoting a much larger story-telling event in my town, I decided to apply and was pleased to be accepted.

When Storytelling Tuesday arrived, James and I got there early but still had a hard time finding two seats together. The event was held in the upstairs billiard room of a popular pub, with at least 100 people present. The vibe in the room was electric.

I fidgeted nervously until it was my turn, feeling significantly more nervous than the previous times I'd shared my story. There were so many people in that room that I was sure at least one person from my church days would be there. Even worse - what if one of them had read my testimony from years ago in Billy Graham's Decision magazine? I feared being publicly chastised for breaking faith and talking about it – but I was resolute in sharing my extimony.

When the emcee announced the title of my talk as "Why I Divorced Religion and Became a None," a wave of laughter ensued. The noisy din of clinking glasses, laughter, and conversation became hushed. When I raised my glass for a sip of water, the audience could see my hand shaking.

"They say that we should speak the truth, even if our voice shakes," I began, "and that is exactly what I am going to do tonight." From that moment, the crowd was with me. They laughed, cried, gasped, and cheered as I shared my sometimes funny, sometimes painful experiences. *See Chapter 9 Resources for the video of my talk at this event.*

When I concluded, the entire audience stood to applaud my courage and my story. People lined up to shake my hand and thank me for sharing what, to many of them, felt like their own story. One woman handed me her business card and told me she'd like to talk with me about including my story in an upcoming anthology she was publishing (Daring to Share: Deception to Truth, by Diana Ryers ©2019 Influence Partners in Publishing). The overwhelming response of that enthusiastic and supportive crowd left me walking on air for several days.

I was excited to share at least some of my story in print, knowing that I could also use the opportunity to tell others about the Divorcing Religion Workshop and another idea I was working on: the Conference on Religious Trauma, or CORT.

Once the Daring to Share anthology was published, I was invited to attend a publicity event with the other authors in another town. James was away visiting his daughters, so I had flown out on my own and would be catching a ride back with one of the other speakers. I was informed on arrival that a latecomer would also be bunking in my hotel room.

Tensions began to rise in our shared room when the other speaker discovered my topic and set about attempting to proselytize (convert) me to Christianity. Adding to my frustration, this woman lived relatively near my own home, and we would be traveling back together in a shared vehicle for many hours.

I did my best, during that long ride home, not to get sucked into the vortex of religious (or as she preferred to call it, "spiritual") conversation she seemed desperate to have. I felt triggered and frustrated by her refusal to simply let me exist as an ex-believer. My feelings shifted, though, when she showed me the cover photo on her cell phone. It was a painting from the vantage point of someone underwater, drowning, looking up at Jesus reaching down from the shore to save them. In that instant, I realized *why* she was so desperate to hold on to her religious faith (and share it with others).

I knew from her own story in the anthology that my travel companion had suffered sexual abuse in childhood, which had saddled her with severe depression.

Upon seeing the painting that was so important to her, I immediately understood that *her mental health hinged on believing that there was a God who loved her*; and, though He failed to protect her as a child (a fact that she ignored), it was His strength that kept her emotional and mental fragility in check as an adult.

This particular religious hook makes me sad and angry, and it is one of the main reasons I especially speak out against Christianity.

It is a disempowering falsehood to believe that humans need a Savior. The source of our power does not lie outside of us; it is altogether internal, and entirely human. We are fully capable of recovering from trauma, addiction, and anything else when we are provided with adequate support and mental health tools – no superstition or "supernatural" help is necessary.

Recognizing this woman's emotional dependence on her faith immediately allowed me to access compassion for her, rather than simply being annoyed by her constant attempts at proselytizing. The rest of the trip was much easier, and I was glad for the epiphany she unknowingly provided through the painting on her phone.

As for sharing my own story at the book launch, it went over well. An old friend from high school surprised me by showing up at the book signing, and it made the night even more special to have the support of one who'd personally witnessed some of my changes. It was thrilling to have audience members ask me to autograph copies of the anthology.

CHAPTER 9 LINKS & RESOURCES

CHAPTER TEN

READY, SET, GROW!

One of the most profound losses to accompany divorcing religion is the loss of a supportive, like-minded community. In my old life, the community was tied to the church. On Sundays, we caught up with each other at services, and through the week we met in homes for Bible studies and small groups. There was also choir, prayer meeting, and even meal trains to help parishioners who were sick or in crisis.

Rebuilding community post-religion is HARD WORK. There is no other way to put it. Time and effort are required, and these resources can be in short supply when one is also struggling with religious trauma.

Thankfully, I found a Meet-Up in my town for people who were interested in building secular lives post-religion. James and I went to the coffee shop advertised and were delighted to meet Tania, who was hosting the Meet-Up. Tania had authored a book called *Alligator Pants: Walking Beyond My Faith*[5] about her own experiences leaving religion, and she invited us to attend a local group for atheists, skeptics, and humanists.

James and I felt welcome at KASHA (Kelowna Atheists, Skeptics, and Humanists Association) from the first time we went, and it became a

---

[5] Kuehn, Tania, *Alligator Pants: Walking Beyond My Faith*, (FriesenPress 2019)

regular part of my life. In addition to semi-monthly forums on various topics, KASHA also offered Skeptics In the Pub, Trivia Nights at a casino, and other opportunities for members to connect. I felt like a parched person crawling out of the desert into an oasis. *See Chapter 10 Resources to learn more about KASHA.*

THE YEAR FROM HELL

In December, James told me that he had been offered his dream job back in Ontario. He had been let go from his local job, though the details he provided were vague. As with the previous job loss, this one was "not his fault." While I had zero interest in moving halfway across the country, I loved James deeply and had built a life with him. My youngest daughter had also opened her heart to James, which was a challenge after Luke's devastation. She opted to join us in our move.

I tearfully informed my mother, brother, oldest daughter, and ex-husband that we would move in late spring of the new year. James accepted his new work position and began moving his things out of our rental. He assured me that he would find acceptable accommodations for us in Ontario once he was settled in at his new job. Until then, he would return to us once a month.

The plan was for my daughter and me to move across the country immediately following the conference I was planning. James assured me that he was meeting regularly with his lawyer and had told his children about our relationship. He even sent photo updates of the suite he was preparing for us in Toronto.

CORT: The CONFERENCE ON RELIGIOUS TRAUMA

Seeing the huge and harmful impact religion has on so many people around the world, in 2019 I decided it was time to put together a conference dedicated to religious trauma. Thanks to my interactions with Dr. Winell and having been a guest on so many religious trauma podcasts, I knew the need was great for such an event to bring together professionals with an interest in religious trauma recovery.

Seeing this need, I founded CORT: *The Conference on Religious Trauma*. Having only ever attended a few conferences in my life (mostly religious ones), I felt sure that I could put on such an event without too much trouble, and I approached it with the zeal and confidence of one who has never undertaken such a task.

I hired an event planner (Heather) and a social media guru (Courtney) to help me get the word out about CORT2020, which was to be the inaugural event. I was entirely caught up in my vision, working full time during the day at my transcription job and then putting in hours every night on preparation and publicity for CORT. Keeping busy prevented me from fretting over our upcoming move.

With Dr. Winell's backing, I successfully solicited the most well-known authors and speakers in the realm of religious trauma to make up the Speaker List for CORT2020, set to take place in beautiful Vancouver, British Columbia in April of 2020.

It was while planning CORT that I came to understand how saturated the mental health field of therapists, counsellors, and social workers is with Christians who believe they are doing God's will. Frequently, they rush to tell me that it's not *their* church/beliefs that cause trauma. Others take offense because I don't provide a platform for religious therapists at my conferences or on my podcast. Still more lament my use of social media to highlight what is wrong with religion instead of what they think is right with it.

I have bumped up against this resistance time and again, even within my own professional governing body, and each time it is a source of frustration. It's not just Christians, either: The mental health field is also rife with New Age adherents, much like I was when I first left the Church. It irritates and confounds me, in professional supervision groups, when my colleagues mention encouraging clients to engage in prayer, consult angels, align their chakras, or explore their "psychic gifts." I consider part of being a professional mental health clinician to include helping my clients accept – and stay grounded in – reality.

Just as it would not be wise for a client struggling with substance misuse to engage with a sponsor who is also misusing substances, it is not wise for clients seeking help to recover from religious trauma to attend church counselling sessions. This is why I endorse the Secular Therapy Project (see Chapter 10 Resources).

HEARTACHE ON HEARTACHE

By early 2020, CORT tickets were selling incredibly well on the website James had created for me. Time was closing in for me to pay the deposit on the hotel banquet room, catering, and other conference-related expenses. Around that same time, I started seeing unsettling videos from China about an unknown virus that seemed to be killing people. I started hearing rumors about a pandemic sweeping the world.

The conference was slated for April of 2020, and several tickets had already been sold. In February, I started feeling genuinely concerned about COVID. I felt frustrated when I was unable to reach James on Valentine's Day. I needed emotional support and possible advice on whether to follow through with the conference. I could not understand why he wasn't answering my Valentine's Day calls, and a familiar feeling returned to the pit of my stomach.

When I finally heard from James, he stated that he had been out hiking with his daughters all day and had no cell phone service. He advised me that, whatever I did, I ought not promise to refund ticket holders. He said that people would understand and that I could not be held liable if there was a pandemic. In general, he expressed the feeling that I was overreacting to the situation.

I was torn trying to decide how to proceed. My mind and heart were set on CORT. I had poured many months into putting this first-of-its-kind event together, but I did not want to risk anyone's safety. At the beginning of March, I made the agonizing decision to postpone CORT.

When I tried to contact James for solace and support, however, I was again unable to reach him. I left several messages on his phone, my stomach churning when he failed to call me back.

On March 7th, I sent him a copy of the email I'd written my speakers alerting them of CORT's postponement. On March 8th, he sent me an email stating that our relationship was over.

I read his email multiple times until it sunk in: Once again, I was being dumped. A strangled cry escaped my throat as I was racked by uncontrollable sobs. "Not again! Not again!" I cried, as my daughter came running to see what was wrong.

I called Courtney and told her what had happened. Immediately, she expressed concern that he might have been up to shady business with the ticket money from CORT, though I could not believe he would do such a thing.

Prizing my professional reputation, I felt it necessary to refund CORT ticket holders; and in doing so, I learned why James had chosen that specific time to end our relationship.

When he had volunteered to set up the CORT website for me, James had assured me that he'd run many conferences before. Inexperienced and trusting (gullible) as I was, it never crossed my mind that he would do anything fraudulent. However, James had set the website up so that all ticket monies went directly into *his* account.

When I postponed the conference and began refunding ticket money, James blocked my access to do so – and blamed me for issuing refunds in the first place. I was then put in the position of publicly declaring what was happening, in an attempt to salvage my professional reputation. In the end, I had to borrow money from relatives and accept donations from strangers to help me pay off ticket holders. My heart and my credibility had been dragged through the mud, but there were more losses to come.

While I tried to come to terms with his shocking financial behavior, I was jolted by an even more bizarre realization: James was still married and had been living a double life with me and my daughter. My entire family had been duped by a con man. Shockingly, *his wife* contacted me a few days following our breakup to say that she had witnessed the entire relationship on social media from the start. She knew that he was deceiving me by living a double life.

When I asked why she hadn't contacted me immediately to let me know of his duplicity, she replied that she thought I must have just been "that type of woman" who enjoys relationships with married men. She informed me that James had taken her and their youngest daughter on tropical vacations during some of his trips home, and that he had been careful not to return with a suntan that would raise my suspicion.

She also said that I wasn't his first victim; he had a pattern of this behavior. To say that I was shocked would be an understatement. I was gutted and emotionally destroyed, and more pain was to come.

BUT WAIT, THERE'S MORE!

Within a week of losing both the conference and my relationship, I received notification from our landlord that we were being evicted because James had been late with paying our rent on three occasions, which is grounds for eviction in British Columbia. While my daughter and I had always provided James with our share of the rent in plenty of time, as the rental unit was in his name, he had neglected to always pay it to the landlord on time – a fact which I was in the dark about.

I now found myself amid a global pandemic, with an immune-compromised daughter and a landlord who wanted to bring multiple strangers through our space to show his property. I was also tasked with finding a suitable new place for us with one less person helping to cover costs.

The situation was almost more than I could bear, mentally and emotionally. Friends and family were deeply concerned for me, and they were right to be. More than once, I thought how easy it would be to inject myself with my daughter's insulin to end my suffering; but I would not do that to my children. I had to keep going.

The one bright spot in my life was that my friend Paul, whom I'd met in Dr. Winell's religious trauma recovery group, heard about my troubles and asked how he could help. His legitimate concern and emotional support helped get me through those dark days.

I knew that some former church friends saw this as God's punishment. My fundamentalist father had told me more than once that he prayed for God to "humble" me and my siblings through calamity, if necessary, to draw us back into the Christian fold.

While I hated my desperate situation, I knew there was nothing supernatural about it. I had made a terrible error in judgment by believing a con man, and it cost me dearly – but I didn't even have time to lament my losses. Deciding in favor of my mental health, I determined that my life would be better without my self-centered, manipulative, fundamentalist father in it. I have not spoken to him since, and it has greatly improved my stress level.

Seeing my impossible rental situation, my mother kindly offered to help me out financially so that I could put a down payment on an older mobile home. I enlisted a realtor, and the search was on. I also had to go through government channels to get the landlord off my back, at least temporarily. Luckily, it was mandated that no landlords could evict during the pandemic.

During those first months of the worldwide pandemic, the real estate market in Canada ground to a halt. No one was sure how long or how deadly COVID would be, so people were hunkering down. There were only a handful of mobile home parks in which I was eligible to purchase, as I was not yet aged 55. In all, only eight mobile homes were for sale in my price range in eligible parks. I went to see all of them and made an offer on one that I liked, even though I wasn't crazy about the park itself.

With my mom's help, financing went through without issue. I was starting to think my situation was turning around – until my realtor contacted me and said she had unbelievable news. For the first time in her lengthy career as a realtor, the mobile home park owner had decided to reject me as a tenant, even with proper financing. For the girl who loves rules, this seemed too crazy to be true.

The realtor had heard through the grapevine that the park's owner was uncomfortable with my outspoken views as an atheist (by then, Google was full of my podcast interviews). The person the realtor heard this from was not willing to go on record, but the result was the same: My hopes came crashing down, and now my timeline was even shorter to find a safe place for me and my disabled daughter to move into.

It is a wonder to me that I did not become an alcoholic through all the emotional upheaval I endured in a short amount of time. I wanted to give up, but that was not an option. I told the realtor to keep looking, and sure enough one more mobile home came on the market. I immediately offered the exact asking price, crossing my fingers. To my tremendous relief, I got the place. Financing was still good, and we were moved in within a couple of weeks. Finally, I could exhale the breath I'd been holding for two months.

ENDINGS AND BEGINNINGS

Even though my daughter and I were now safe in our very own home, I felt battered, pummelled, and drained. Tears were a regular occurrence, and I'd had to go down to part-time hours doing transcription as I tried to piece myself back together emotionally. Fragile would be an accurate description. While many urged me to take James to Small Claims Court to try and force him to pay back the money he'd stolen, I just did not have the energy. I had nothing left emotionally - no reserves and no hope. I was strictly in survival mode.

Paul had become a dear friend and ardent supporter, and we visited almost daily over video. Sometimes, all I could do was cry – and all he could do was witness my pain and encourage me to let it out. I felt safe with him not just because he was already a friend, but because he was compassionate and wise, too.

I appreciated being able to show him my ugly cry with no fear of judgment. During our video calls, I could cry, curse, and pour out my sorrows. He listened like a true friend, offering to help however he could. During our monthly participation in a group conference call for those recovering from RTS (courtesy of Dr. Winell), I had always admired this man for his wisdom, compassion, and dignity. I felt extremely fortunate to count him as my friend. His presence in my life as I processed deep feelings of betrayal, anger, and grief was a great comfort to me, and I let him know.

In 2021, Paul traveled from Mississippi to visit me in British Columbia. His steadfast friendship meant so much, and bit by bit our friendship blossomed. He had shown himself to be trustworthy, dependable, and a huge supporter of my efforts. Since we both understood religious trauma and knew each other's back story, it was easy to be our authentic selves together. At some point, our attraction became undeniable; but I was still recovering from heartbreak and also had some hesitancy around our age difference, with Paul being 22 years my senior. Ever the gentleman, Paul accepted my request to keep our friendship platonic while I continued to process my grief.

After being in my new place for a few months and back at my transcription job full time, I decided the time was right to resume planning for CORT — only now, it would be for CORT2021, as an online event.

Never having held an online conference, I reached out to a man I knew who had recently popped up in the religious trauma realm. He assured me that he had hosted many online conferences and would be just the right person to help with my event, too. When he sent me a video of himself hosting one of his conferences, however, I knew that we would not be a good fit. When I told him so, he proved my concerns about his character to be correct: He stole my conference idea and began promoting his own "e-Conference on Religious Trauma."

When others alerted me to his plans, I immediately reached out and asked him to change the name of his event. In response, he threatened to sue me. Still catching my breath from the damage to my business and my heart in 2020, I decided it would be best for my mental health to simply cut ties with this man and do my best to put on an excellent conference.

Having learned my lesson, I reconnected with both my original event planner and my social media guru. Together, we set our sights on May 2021 for CORT. I checked in with my speakers and resumed giving podcast interviews to highlight our event. Before I knew it, we were going full speed ahead with preparations for the now-online event.

When I began advertising CORT back in 2019, I had no idea what the interest level would be. I didn't know if I could even sell 50 tickets. In the end, the inaugural event stretched over five days and included more than 20 speakers – and I sold over 300 tickets! It was a resounding success.

My friends at KASHA supported my work and wanted it to be successful. They knew what had happened with James, and they offered friendship and encouragement. I became a board member and eventually was asked to serve as vice president.

Encouraged by the high turnout for CORT2021, I immediately began working on CORT2022, which was held the next spring. It was obvious that CORT struck a chord amongst both therapists and members of the general public who were recovering from RTS. As more and more people were leaving churches in the USA, particularly with the rise of Donald Trump and the Q-Anon cult splitting Christian families apart, people were hungry to learn more about their religious trauma and how they could potentially recover.

Recognizing that one particularly toxic aspect of RTS related to sexuality, I decided to put together an additional event for October of 2022 called *Shameless Sexuality: Life After Purity Culture*. This event would be entirely about Purity Culture recovery, including all things related to sex and sexuality. People again showed great interest, and I knew such a conference would meet a need and allow me to serve this worthy demographic in a meaningful way.

In the summer of 2022, I traveled to the southern United States to visit with Paul and meet his adult children and grandchildren. This, my first time in that part of the USA, felt shockingly different from Canada.

Peace and Justice Memorial Center in Montogomery, Alabama

We paid an emotional visit to the Peace and Justice Memorial Center in Montogomery, Alabama, where Paul laid roses at each memorial where a lynching had taken place in a county where he had lived or worked.

Not only did I see a new level of poverty in the deep South, but billboards assaulted me with threats of Hell if I didn't go to church, and massive crosses erected along the highways loomed as an ever-present reminder that Jesus was watching.

Traumatizing sign I saw in Alabama

I sucked in my breath each time I saw a Confederate flag flying in someone's yard, and I did my best not to snipe at cashiers who told me to "Have a blessed day!" while handing me my purchases. Such intense religiosity at a place of business made me feel very far away from Canada.

During that trip, Paul asked me to marry him, which I happily did in July of that same year. As my daughter's health issues preclude us from living in the USA, Paul moved to Canada and now shares our home.

Two happy atheists, married on a Canadian mountaintop

Every day, we go birdwatching (he is a retired wildlife biologist for the US government), enjoy the beautiful scenery, and share life's ups and downs as those in recovery from religious trauma. I did not know I could feel so deeply connected to and cherished by another. Paul is an honorable person, and I am proud to be his partner.

In October of that year, I was proud to host the inaugural Shameless Sexuality conference online, followed in December by co-facilitating one of Dr. Winell's religious trauma recovery retreats, this time in Massachusetts.

Postcards I handed out at our local Pride event advertising the Shameless Sexuality Conference

In 2022, I also added Podcast Host to my list of accomplishments, as I launched the Divorcing Religion Podcast - as well as the Conference on Religious Trauma YouTube channel, which is now the Divorcing Religion YouTube channel. The podcast started with a real bang as I had the pleasure of interviewing well-known atheists like Seth Andrews (The Thinking Atheist), Hemant Mehta (The Friendly Atheist), and Matt Dillahunty.

Star-struck meeting Seth Andrews, The Thinking Atheist

I was delighted to finally meet Seth Andrews (The Thinking Atheist) in person when we were both speakers at the Western Canadian Reason Conference in 2023. He is as nice in person as he is on his show.

Hemant Mehta, The Friendly Atheist

Atheist activist Matt Dillahunty

Interviewing well-revered atheists like Seth Andrews, Hemant Mehta, and Matt Dillahunty put the Divorcing Religion Podcast on the map from the start. Dr. Darrel Ray, founder of Recovering from Religion, has also been a frequent guest and strong supporter of my podcast and events, for which I am grateful.

In 2023, I continued building my private counselling and coaching practice focused on religious trauma recovery. The Divorcing Religion podcast gained momentum, and CORT was a success once again. I felt proud that year when Dr. Winell also asked me to work as an affiliate religious trauma recovery coach for Journey Free

Late in 2023, Paul and I watched an adaptation of Margaret Atwood's story The Handmaid's Tale (McClellan and Stewart, Houghton Mifflin, 1985; Cape 1985). Having escaped fundamentalism myself, the story resonated uncomfortably closely with me. To my amazement, Paul mentioned that he had gone birdwatching with Margaret Atwood and her late husband, Graeme Gibson, more than once in the 1980s - and that he had even *stayed at their home* in Toronto!

Seeing a fantastic opportunity, I reached out to Ms. Atwood immediately with an interview request. Inside a card featuring a gorgeous hummingbird (created by First Nations artist Lon French), I wrote how much *The Handmaid's Tale* meant to me as a former fundamentalist Christian woman. I also included a photo of Paul and conveyed his fond regards to her.

The card I mailed to Margaret Atwood

I was floored when Ms. Atwood's assistant informed me that Margaret would be delighted to join me as a guest on the Divorcing Religion podcast! *For a link to this special episode, see Chapter 10 Resources*

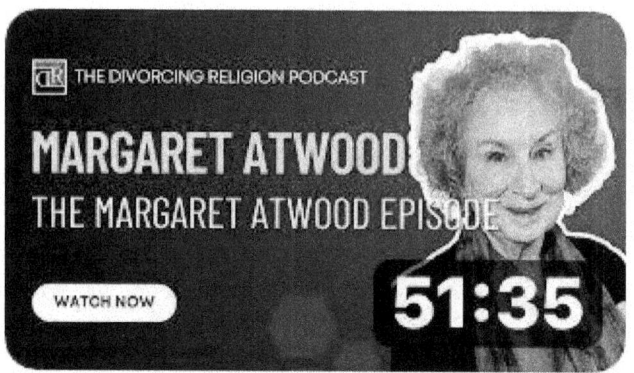

Icon Margaret Atwood, author and environmentalist

In April of 2024, Paul and I were thrilled to visit Stockholm, Sweden, for the cinematic premiere of *Leaving Jesus* (Ellen Fiske, Momento Film 2024), a documentary filmed at several of Dr. Marlene Winell's San Francisco retreats between 2018 and 2022. We both appear in the documentary, with Paul featured prominently.

We were delighted when director Ellen Fiske and director of photography, Pia Lehto, filmed our beautiful outdoor wedding in 2022 as they were finishing up our interviews for *Leaving Jesus*. We treasure our friendship with these two powerful European women who are shining a light on religious trauma, so we jumped at the chance to show them our support. Plus, visiting Sweden let me check an item off my bucket list: Visiting The ABBA Museum!

Paul in front of *Leaving Jesus* posters in Stockholm

Paul, Ellen, Janice, and Pia celebrating after filming our wedding

On our first day in Stockholm, where we had never been before, we were trying to find out which train would take us to our hotel. We stopped at one of the subway stations to ask for directions, and the young woman behind the counter became very animated upon seeing us. She ran around to the front of her desk and cried "I know you! I just saw you in a movie at the film festival!" and proceeded to give Paul a great big hug. It was a fantastic welcome to Sweden and tremendous validation that the world is ready to learn about Religious Trauma Syndrome.

It was a pleasure reconnecting with friends from across North America and Europe whom we'd met at Dr. Winell's retreats, and who had also flown to Sweden for the documentary premiere. We toured the movie studio and met with many who had worked hard behind the scenes to bring the story to life on the big screen. In addition to attending the gala premiere, we were guests on a popular Swedish podcast and attended several screenings where we participated in Question-and-Answer periods after each show.

**Dr. Marlene Winell and Janice Selbie
in Stockholm for the Leaving Jesus premier**

The documentary was well-received everywhere, and we felt honored to be there. We look forward to *Leaving Jesus* being released in North America sometime soon.

As of 2024, I am happy to share that:

- I am now the acting president of KASHA: Kelowna's Atheists, Skeptics, and Humanists Association,
- Having served his sentence, my nephew is working hard and thriving,
- I continue to enjoy a deep friendship with my former husband,
- My daughters are now free-thinking adults with whom I share a loving relationship, and
- My still-Christian mother remains one of my greatest supporters.

Sisters

CHAPTER 10 LINKS & RESOURCES

CHAPTER ELEVEN

CLIENT STORIES

MY CLIENTS ARE PEOPLE JUST LIKE YOU

My religious trauma clients come from a variety of religious, ethnic, and professional backgrounds. I've worked with people aged 19 to 83 across North America, the United Kingdom, Europe, New Zealand, Australia, Chile, India, Japan, the Middle East, and West Africa. My clients include teachers, police officers, soldiers, strippers, psychologists, musicians, actors, authors, comedians, sex workers, stay-at-home parents, former clergy, senior citizens, IT specialists, restaurant servers, cashiers, and construction workers.

Religious backgrounds of people I've worked with include Amish, Baptist, Buddhist, Catholic, Christian and Missionary Alliance, Christian Orthodox, Christian Science, Church of Christ, Church of God, Dutch Reformed, Episcopal, Evangelical, Foursquare, Hindu, IHOP (International House of Prayer), Independent Fundamental Baptist, Islam, Jehovah's Witness, Judaism, Lutheran, Mormon, Nazarene, Presbyterian, Scientology, Seventh Day Adventist, Unification Church, Vineyard, various Yoga cults, and more.

CLIENT STORIES

The following stories were inspired by my clients. No real names have been used, and the stories are a compilation of clients from similar backgrounds.

CHRISTINA

Growing up in a Jehovah's Witness (JW) family, Christina's parents were rigid, authoritarian, and deeply controlling. Like other JW children, she was not permitted to make friends with non-JW kids. Public school felt painful and humiliating for Christina, as she was not permitted to participate in any classroom celebrations for birthdays or holidays. She could not even color Easter eggs with her classmates. She dreaded being forced to go door-to-door proselytizing and potentially coming face-to-face with a classmate.

From an early age, Christina was taught that nonbelievers were dangerous, as was the entire world outside the Kingdom Hall. Rather than a fun and exhilarating time of exploration, her childhood and adolescence were drudgery.

She was terrified of Armageddon and believed it would happen before she grew up. In fact, she was surprised when she reached the height where she could see over top of the kitchen microwave. Abusive disciplinarians, Christina's parents hit her with shoes, belts, and hairbrushes. Sometimes they forced her to kneel on uneven surfaces as a form of their twisted discipline, even when she did not know what rule she'd broken.

When Christina's older sibling ran away, her parents became even more controlling. She was only permitted to leave home to attend school or the Kingdom Hall. Christina had not one friend and felt isolated and depressed. Against her wishes, Christina agreed to be baptized in her early teen years, to get her parents off her back.

To remain abstinent until marriage, Christina was pressured to marry young. At 18, she wed a boy from her congregation. As is typical amongst JWs, the young couple was discouraged from pursuing higher education and encouraged to devote all time and energy to winning new converts.

Christina contacted me in her 30s. She and her husband no longer attend regular services (a practice known as "fading") but they do not want to make an official break, as they fear being entirely shunned by their families. The couple feels angry about being raised in a high-demand religion, scared of being completely isolated, and trapped in dead-end jobs since they did not attend college. We are currently working on acceptance, boundaries, and communication.

ZEB

Zeb grew up in a large, devout Mormon family. As far as he knows, he is the first one in several generations to reject being a member of the LDS (Latter-Day Saints) community.

While Zeb's parents are not polygamous, they are deeply entrenched in the church and proud of their family history. He grew up hearing stories of his pioneering family. To please his parents, Zeb memorized his family tree and verses from the Book of Mormon.

From a young age, Zeb felt that he was different. With the onset of adolescence, he recognized his attraction to other young men in the congregation but never dared tell anyone.

Zeb was baptized at 8 years old. Practically every other person he knew was also Mormon. In his early 20s, he spent two years as a missionary in Africa. Though he fought against it, Zeb developed romantic feelings towards his fellow male missionary, which he kept to himself. After returning home from his mission work, Zeb was instructed to find a young Mormon woman and get married immediately.

Living in another country exposed Zeb to other cultures and belief systems, leading him to doubt the religion he was indoctrinated into from birth. He began to resent the pressures placed on him his whole life and wanted time and space to re-evaluate his life.

Eventually, Zeb's parents asked why he was not finding a wife. When he came out to them as gay and a nonbeliever, his parents were shocked and urged him to reconsider. When their shock turned to anger, Zeb decided to move out of their house and leave Utah altogether.

I heard from Zeb in his late 20s, when we began unpacking his Purity Culture indoctrination and other religious trauma. Today, he is happily married to his husband and tentatively re-opening communication lines with his parents. Two of Zeb's siblings have also recently rejected Mormonism and credit him as a courageous trailblazer.

JANELLE

Janelle and her siblings had an overbearing Christian fundamentalist mother and a father who was on the road most of the time for his job. Janelle's mother insisted on "homeschooling" all 8 of her children, though she provided little education past about a third-grade level. Utterly disdainful of government interference, Janelle's mother gave birth at home each time and did not obtain birth certificates for any of her children, nor any vaccinations.

Janelle's mother instructed the children in the basics of reading and math, only. At that point, the children were essentially left to their own devices. Janelle's school days were filled with caring for younger siblings, rather than learning about and exploring the world around her. Since her parents doled out extreme punishment for minor infractions, Janelle made it her mission to try and protect the younger children, often taking the blame and punishment so they did not have to.

Sadly, a man at church molested Janelle and one of her sisters. Steeped in patriarchy and misogyny, the girls were not believed by their mother and essentially had no one else to tell. They had no friends and no teachers checking in on them. The patriarchal power structure was reinforced at their tiny fundamentalist church alongside Purity Culture indoctrination, leaving Janelle to question whether she had, in some way, provoked the man's abuse.

In her teens, Janelle started sneaking out and met a boy who was kind and caring. Eventually, she ran away and married him. Her husband supported Janelle as she made her first trips to see a dentist. Eventually she felt comfortable attending on her own and even received braces for her teeth.

Though she was able to escape Homeschool Hell, Janelle struggled with low self-esteem, particularly related to her lack of education. We addressed this issue, as well as those related to Purity Culture indoctrination and personal identity. After several sessions with me, Janelle's self-confidence increased. She is currently a full-time college student interested in social work.

PETER

Peter was born to missionary parents whose job was to translate the Bible into foreign languages. As was usual for parents who worked at their Mission, the children were sent off to boarding school in another country at the age of 6. Boarding school was a terrifying and lonely experience for Peter, who internalized early on that he was more of a nuisance to his parents than anything else.

His parents' slave-like devotion to Jesus, the Christian Gospel, and their Mission Board meant that Peter was far down on their priority list. When a male teacher at the boarding school began abusing Peter, he tried telling his mother what was going on. Instead of contacting the school, she reprimanded Peter for lying and threatened not to let him come home over the holiday if he brought it up again.

The boarding school is now under the spotlight for multiple sexual abuse allegations brought forward by many former students.

As an adult, Peter reached out to me for help with religious trauma and toxic Purity Culture beliefs that robbed him of sexual enjoyment. Now into the second half of his life, he had never had a romantic relationship or even been on a date.

Peter eventually determined that he did not wish to maintain contact with his mother, as she still refused to believe him about being abused at school. With my support, Peter continues to explore his autonomy and his sexuality. He recently developed a profile on a dating site and has been enjoying interacting with others.

SARAH

Sarah grew up in a non-religious home with parents who suffered from addictions. Her father was an alcoholic and her mother was a workaholic. When her older sister got pregnant at 16, Sarah felt like she had become invisible. Emotionally neglected and largely ignored, Sarah was ripe pickings for a cult once she moved away to attend college.

After an intense campaign of love-bombing, the group denied her time to consider the veracity of their teachings and applied constant pressure for her to reject her family and the rest of the world. In a few weeks, Sarah gave up her dream of becoming a teacher. She dropped out of school, abandoned her apartment, and moved onto the cult compound.

Once there, the cult leader insisted that Sarah hand over her cell phone and cease all contact with outsiders, including friends and family. Lack of sleep, insufficient food, and constant pressure from the group ensured her quick conformity to life on the compound. The cult leader gave her a new name and started to control every aspect of Sarah's life.

After six years inside the cult, Sarah gathered her courage to make a break for it, literally fleeing in the middle of the night. She was able to reconnect with her family and resume her education. After graduating, Sarah booked a trip to India – where she ended up getting hooked by a yoga cult. This time, she figured out within one year that it was a cult and left immediately.

Sarah reached out to me because she was concerned that she had twice fallen into high-demand groups. She wanted to discover her blind spots and understand what had made her vulnerable. We spent time exploring how beliefs and identities form and recognizing the hallmarks and tactics of high-demand groups. Sarah also participated in the Divorcing Religion Workshop, which has an entire module devoted to recognizing and avoiding fundamentalist thinking.

HELEN

Helen's parents raised her and her younger siblings in Eastern Canada in a Roman Catholic cult. They lived on a compound out in the countryside, with other families who were in the cult. Three times daily, they were required to attend Mass on the compound. The children all attended classes in a one-room schoolhouse on the property, until about grade eight.

At that point, girls were sent home to focus entirely on homemaking skills. The exception was if a girl wanted to become a nun, in which case they were permitted to continue their education off campus in a religious setting. Helen loved learning but did not want to become a nun.

Though she had frequent headaches and poor vision, Helen was never taken for an eye exam. Instead of modern medicine, the cult believed in the power of prayer and fasting as a viable healing alternative. Helen did not visit a medical doctor or dentist until she was an adult.

Helen's cousin, who lived with her family, began displaying signs of violent psychosis in his early teens. His psychotic episodes tended to focus on religious themes, during which he spoke with tremendous authority and zeal. Sometimes the whole family was afraid of him.

When her cousin nearly strangled her to death during a psychotic episode, Helen knew she had to leave. Without saying a word to anyone, she planned her escape and headed for western Canada, where she had an estranged older family member. Thankfully, they took Helen in immediately.

As mentioned, Helen had never seen a doctor. She also had never had a bank account and had no identification. Her family member patiently and gently exposed Helen to life in the real world, including getting eyeglasses. To Helen's delight, her chronic headaches diminished once she started wearing glasses. She was soon taking GED courses to complete her high school education.

Helen found me through the Divorcing Religion podcast. While she has made tremendous strides, she struggles with nightmares of being back in the cult and of going to Hell, which was a large part of the cult's teaching. Socially, Helen feels that she never quite fits in or is an imposter on the verge of being found out.

Helen most enjoys the inner child work we do together, where she gets to lovingly reparent herself. We continue working on acceptance, values clarification, and developing her own identity.

AMRAM

Amram was the fourth-born child in an ultra-Orthodox Jewish family. He has seven siblings. What defines Amram's childhood and adolescence are rules, rules, and more rules. What he ate, how he dressed, and with whom he could associate were all dictated by his family's religion and culture. Amram never knew anyone from outside of his group until he was in his 30s.

Amram did everything his parents and religious community demanded of him. His education was comprised entirely of religious training, with little thought given to anything else. His role was to become a religious scholar, though he would have preferred a life built around art.

From a young age, Amram loved to draw and create. This was tolerated in his childhood but frowned on as a teen. Starting in adolescence, he felt the need to hide this beautiful aspect of himself. Chafing beneath the load of rules and expectations he had no say in, Amram yearned for the freedom to live his own life – even though it would cost him all he had ever known.

At age 35, Amram reached out to me for support as he explored the strange new world he escaped into, one without rules governing every aspect of his life. He was vulnerable and mourning significant losses but thrilled by the freedom he had never known. He knew he could ask me questions about anything and he would always receive a kind and forthright answer. We tackled issues related to grief and loss, identity exploration, and building a safe and supportive secular community.

JAYDEN

Jayden refers to himself as an atheist and recovering Evangelical. He grew up attending a "nondenominational" charismatic Christian church and school. He recalls questioning his parents' beliefs in childhood and being chastised in both Sunday school and Christian school for "doubting." He recalls being forced to pray and lying to his parents and others about his nonbelief. To Jayden, his parents' love for him and his siblings felt entirely conditional upon them embracing Christianity.

When he was in primary school, Jayden's dad believed he was "called" to become a pastor. The family finances became severely stretched when his dad quit his job and went to Bible college. Jayden felt embarrassed by never being the first to own anything, from used bikes to used shoes. When Christmas came, he knew better than to ask for anything special. His parents believed that enjoyment was to be had in Heaven rather than on Earth.

While his parents did not physically abuse Jayden or his siblings, they would stop talking to their children as punishment and insist that all siblings ignore the child being punished. Masturbation and anything related to sexuality were considered sinful, and he recalled his parents removing the door to his bedroom during adolescence if they thought he might be doing something they did not like.

After graduating high school, Jayden wanted to attend a secular college. His parents were dismayed and told him they would not offer any help unless he attended a Christian school. By then, Jayden had been able to access podcasts, documentaries, and articles on the internet that cemented his nonbelief. He packed a bag and left his parent's home and has not returned.

I started working with Jayden in his middle 20s when he felt ready to do some work related to Purity Culture indoctrination and potentially resuming contact with his parents. He wanted help with boundaries and communication tactics with still-religious family members. Jayden lives with his girlfriend and they are considering attending an upcoming milestone wedding anniversary of his parents.

KC

KC contacted me in their early 20s after their parents rejected KC's nonbinary status and insisted they move out of the family home so as not to influence younger siblings. KC grew up in "the church without a name," sometimes referred to as Two-by-Twos or The Truth.

In KC's family, their father's word was law. They had no TV or stereo and were expected to participate in daily readings, by their father, from the King James Bible. At various times, KC's parents attempted to cast out demons from KC and his siblings, terrifying all of the children.

The Two-by-Twos don't have churches or pastors. Instead, "workers" travel and stay in the homes of other members. Sadly, KC and some of his siblings were molested by workers through the years. KC's parents refused to believe them and punished them for "speaking ill of a brother."

KC began sneaking out of the house in their middle teens to meet up with kids from school. KC hated feeling like an outcast, especially not understanding any references to popular TV, movies, or music.

KC and I talk about whatever is on their mind when we meet. Some days, it is about catching up on pop culture; others it is about forming healthy bonds. KC is not sure where they fall on the spectrum of belief. We explore critical thinking skills and red flags where ideologies and relationships are concerned. At times, they express intense anger over how controlling their parents were, as well as how much KC sometimes misses feeling safe within the rigid boundaries of their parents' belief system.

ALI

Ali is from a staunchly Muslim country. He took great care contacting me because he would be in grave danger if his family or community discovered that he was no longer religious. His daily life included constantly checking over his shoulder and having to lie and participate in prayers multiple times in order not to arouse suspicion.

Ali found me through the Divorcing Religion Podcast. After watching several episodes, he courageously set up a consultation. Though scared, he was relieved to share his secret atheism. There was always an element of danger when we spoke, and I felt very nervous for him.

Eventually, Ali told me that he could no longer stay in his country. In addition to his well-grounded fears of being labeled an infidel, his conscience insisted that he make a run for freedom instead of pretending allegiance to a religion he did not believe. He also abhorred the thought of handing over his future daughters for the forced genital mutilation practiced in his culture.

We discussed the dangers of relying on smugglers and practiced grounding exercises for the high-anxiety situations that awaited him. Mostly, Ali just needed a safe person to share his fears and dreams with. He wanted at least one other person to know what he was about to undertake and to provide emotional support.

I was honored to be that person for Ali, and I felt tremendously relieved to hear from him when he arrived in another country. He experienced violence and robbery along his journey, but he is now safe and working with authorities to secure his place in his new homeland. We continue to meet online for sessions whenever he needs to check in.

MY INVITATION TO YOU

If you recognize aspects of your own situation in any of my client compilation stories, or if you are wondering if you might be a victim of religious trauma, I can help. You can connect with me or book and pay for a session directly through **my website:** https://www.divorcing-religion.com/

I would love to hear your thoughts on the Memoir portion of my book or chat with you about being a guest on the Divorcing Religion podcast. Reach out to me at Janice@divorcing-religion.com.

You can also visit **my YouTube channel** for fantastic videos from CORT, the Shameless Sexuality Conference, and the Divorcing Religion Podcast here: YouTube.com/@cometocort

IN CLOSING

You have now completed the Memoir portion of this book. I hope you found it educational, encouraging, and even entertaining. The next portion is the Survival Handbook, complete with questions and opportunities for personal reflection.

The pain and trauma of losing my religious identity, community, and belief system closely resembled the pain and trauma of losing my marriage partnership of nearly two decades. What started off feeling strong and hopeful, with the confidence to weather any storm, dissolved around me and slipped away like sand through an hourglass. Feeling confused, lost, and very much alone, I dreaded running into people who had known me before, not wanting them to see my new solo situation of pain and uncertainty.

The following Divorcing Religion Survival Handbook is my gift to you, written by a professional counsellor who has a personal understanding of marital breakdown and divorce - and a personal understanding of faith loss and how to build a healthy secular life post-religion.

For the greatest benefit, sign up to participate in my online Divorcing Religion Workshop. The workshop, facilitated by me, has helped many other people - and it can help you, too.

Resources can be accessed from the Divorcing Religion website using the QR code here and at the end of each module.

CLIENT STORIES

CHAPTER 11 LINKS & RESOURCES

Divorcing Religion

A Survival Handbook

Finding Freedom from Fundamentalism

Janice Selbie, RPC

©2024

SECTION TWO: WORKBOOK

WELCOME

WELCOME to the Divorcing Religion Survival Handbook, a guide to help you explore where you came from, figure out where you are now, and set your sights on where you want to be.

Before we get started, please note that indoctrination does not only occur within religious spheres. Any ideology and community can become extreme, including those that are religious/spiritual, political, nutritional, or environmental. Many of the clients I support around religious trauma syndrome are also coming to terms with losing their parents or other loved ones to the relatively new Q-Anon and Trump cults that have arisen over the past few years.

Those raised in religious homes may be swayed by conspiracy theories or drawn down other cult-type rabbit holes more easily because they have already been primed to swap logic for magical thinking by way of belief in things supernatural and miraculous. When we decide to suspend critical thought for one circumstance, it is easier to do so again. Additionally, even if we hated the rigid rules and lack of autonomy in our former groups, authoritarianism can feel comfortable if it is what we're familiar with.

Please practice self-care as you work your way through this section of the book. Be sure to take plenty of breaks. Go for a walk, drink a glass of water, call a friend to chat. The Handbook will be here waiting, ready when you are, to continue.

Just like the end of a marriage, divorce from your once-loved religion feels painful, exhausting, and confusing. The loss and grief are real. The good news is, just as life after marital divorce exists, life also continues after Divorcing Religion - and it can be a life more authentic and rewarding than you have ever experienced.

As with romantic divorce, Divorcing Religion proceeds through stages, which I have broken down into the 7 components listed in the Table of Contents. To reap the most benefit from this Survival Handbook, take your time to read (and re-read) each module and do the recommended homework. You will get out of it what you put into it. Be willing to explore your experiences and beliefs, viewing them under the microscope of scrutiny. Only then will you be able to understand, grieve, release, and rebuild.

INTRODUCTION

It's easy to get swept up in the hope and guidance provided by religion. The truly hard part comes when you realize you no longer feel the same way about it - and you must abandon your faith. Or perhaps, your faith has abandoned you.

Religion is often used to control the behavior of others, and it always comes with a cost for adherents. In a 2011 series of published articles in the professional journal "Cognitive Behavior Therapy Today," American Psychologist Dr. Marlene Winell describes **"Religious trauma syndrome" (RTS)** as a set of symptoms and characteristics related to harmful experiences with religion. Dr. Winell points out that these symptoms and characteristics are the result of two things: Immersion in a controlling religion, and the impact of leaving a religious group.[6]

Religious fundamentalism distorts our view of self, others, and the world around us by imposing a black-or-white, binary, fearful view. Think of a preschool child on the playground, happily interacting with children from every possible background. The child has not yet internalized their parents' conditions about what and who is acceptable to love; they have not yet been fully indoctrinated.

Without our consent, our caregivers can impose and subjugate us to fit the mold of their own beliefs. If we converted in adulthood, we imposed these beliefs and standards upon ourselves.

Regardless of how we became entangled in fundamentalism, **our power lies in our ability to now choose what we believe.** By reading this Survival Handbook and thoughtfully completing the exercises, you are already exercising that power. Knowing this, I want you to proceed with self-love and self-acceptance to the best of your ability.

Whether we were indoctrinated during childhood or converted as an adult, religion provided us with a sense of purpose, a community, and an identity. Being part of an insular religious group also provided us with security, comfort, and a particular worldview that was not entirely based on fact.

In general, fundamentalist groups:

- strictly adhere to dogma
- emphasize in-group and out-group distinctions

---

[6] Winell, M. (2011) Religious Trauma Syndrome (Series of 3 articles), Cognitive Behavioural Therapy Today, Vol. 39, Issue 2, May 2011, Vol. 39, Issue 3, September 2011, Vol. 39, Issue 4, November 2011. British Association of Behavioural and Cognitive Therapies, London. The articles can be accessed here: https://www.journeyfree.org/rts/

- place a heavy emphasis on the purity of the group and its adherents
- discourage secular education and relationships outside of the group (except to make new converts)
- strongly resist change and have a pronounced yearning for times past.

Additionally, fundamentalist groups place large demands on the resources of group members' money, time, and energy.

MODULE ONE

BREAKING UP IS HARD TO DO:
Realizing it's over

This module challenges you to accept what has occurred so that you can begin to build your new life.

HOW DID YOU AND RELIGION MEET?

In the Memoir portion of this book, I shared about my childhood indoctrination into Evangelical Christianity, and how my parents believed that the Bible was the literal and inerrant word of God. Not wanting to disappoint them kept me bound to their belief system. Determined to keep the faith, I tied myself into a mental pretzel trying to force all the pieces to fit when they didn't make sense.

It's important to recognize how religion became such a big part of our lives. Understanding this can aid in building our self-compassion.

If we were introduced to religion in our childhood (or even during adolescence), we lacked the critical thinking abilities required to make an informed decision. If the person who introduced us to religion was our caregiver, we had no option to do anything other than embrace what they offered us, since *our survival depended on them and keeping them happy.* Even if we were not "scared" into believing, we certainly were under innate, subconscious, psychological pressure (i.e., coercion) to please our caregivers.

Likewise, if we met religion during adolescence, an element of emotional pressure and conformity probably came along with it, in addition to our own natural state of immaturity. Pressuring a child or adolescent to make a "life-long" decision is immoral and unkind.

Adults who become religious usually do so during a state of flux or transition. Often, adults turn to religious groups when in the throes of an identity crisis, addiction, divorce, poverty, lack of community support, feeling marginalized, poor self-esteem, etc.

Who introduced you to religion? What was their role in your life? What stage of life were you in at that time?

_____

_____

Whether your breakup with religion came suddenly or over time, the result is the same: **Your assumptive worldview dissolves, and you are forced to start over.** If you were raised in your religion, you will likely have fallout from relatives. If your partner still believes, things may get extremely uncomfortable. But you cannot simply force yourself, or will yourself, to believe what no longer makes sense. I know because I tried.

As Oliver Wendell Holmes stated long ago: "One's mind, once stretched by a new idea, never regains its original dimensions."

Do you remember when the *seed of doubt* was planted in your brain? As a diehard believer, I worked hard to keep my beliefs reinforced. All of my friends were also fundamentalists; and the only books, sermons, and music I allowed in my life were those designed to point me back to Jesus, should questions arise.

I was skilled at glossing over Bible portions that made me uncomfortable (such as Abraham preparing to murder his son, Lot offering his daughters to a gang, etc.), and defending my faith via circular reasoning using Bible verses as answers. Having been in the Church since birth, I was fully indoctrinated – and I did my best to indoctrinate my kids, too.

But there came a time when a seed of doubt was planted. It slipped into a dark, tiny crack, where it germinated. As fundamentalists, we imposed self-judgment (and incurred the judgment of others) for the very act of questioning. But it is the act of questioning that sets us free from our fundamentalist thinking! *Doubt in a belief becomes the crack necessary to expand our perception; it is the seed that is necessary for our growth.*

My marriage was fertile ground for this doubt, as I simply could not accept the mandate that I, an autonomous adult, was to obey all of my husband's decisions. **Resentment was my seed of doubt.**

Why must I obey another adult simply because he was born with a different set of genitalia? Why was I not permitted to think for myself, and behave accordingly?

Your seed of doubt may be the notion of Hell, lack of scientific evidence, demand for tithing, or unloving hypocrites in the pews or pulpit.

For many of my religious trauma clients in the USA, their massive seed of doubt was when Donald Trump was endorsed by Christians for the office of President.

When COVID arrived, churches and pastors denying scientific and medical advice and putting vulnerable persons at risk by refusing to wear masks was a seed of doubt too big for many to ignore.

What was the seed of doubt that started your journey of Divorcing Religion?

_____

_____

At first, I tried to stifle my doubt. I prayed more, read my Bible more, continued attending services, and diligently put on my head-covering every day. I hoped that my resentment would disappear if I could only receive a greater anointing of God's Holy Spirit. As earnest as my seeking was, it was to no avail. Like a beach ball held beneath the water too long, I was about to break free from the deadweight of fundamentalism.

Many of us raised in fundamentalism saw no worthy future apart from attending a religious college and becoming a pastor or missionary, or the wife of a pastor or missionary. Indoctrination is thorough and easy when we are raised in a religious environment and not permitted to associate with unbelievers. Homeschooling can add significantly to this isolation.

How long were you religious before you started having doubts?

_____

_____

"Should I Stay or Should I Go" is an agonizing phase in any relationship. It is the point where you realize that there is a significant problem, but the thought of leaving is too painful. You are willing to overlook virtually any flaw to avoid the pain and loss of leaving.

Humans go to great lengths to try and alleviate their **cognitive dissonance** (the psychological discomfort we experience upon learning new information that challenges a deeply held belief) so that they can remain in familiar surroundings.

How long did you continue attending services after doubts crept in?

_____

_____

The above question is significant because it can indicate the depth of our investment in a belief. The Cambridge Dictionary defines **sunk cost fallacy** as: "The idea that a company or organization is more likely to continue with a project if they have already invested a lot of money, time, or effort in it, even when continuing is not the best thing to do."

You can see how this translates into the realm of religion - or virtually any other significant ideological attachment.

Abrahamic religions, in particular, saddle adherents with the *turnstile effect*, making it easy to gain entry to the group but very hard to leave. Those brave enough to depart suffer significant losses.

What kept you hanging on to your beliefs (family, work/ministry, ego, etc.)?

_____

_____

When we realize something is amiss in our fundamentalist belief system, it has a profound cascading effect. While questions assail us, grief settles over us like a shroud, bringing uncomfortable and inconvenient emotions:

Shock: How could I have believed this?

Confusion: Is any of it true? What DO I believe?

Fear: What if I'm wrong? Are my other beliefs also untrue? Can I find another job outside the religious setting?

Anger: What am I supposed to do now? I have given so much time, energy, and money to this belief! How could I have believed it for so long?

Sadness and Guilt: How do I tell my partner/parents/children?

In this initial phase of Divorcing Religion, you may bounce back and forth between:

Bargaining (It's not that bad; maybe I can keep attending for my spouse/kids)

Denial (Something feels wrong, but it can't be my beliefs. It must be me),

Depression (Loss of community, identity, and worldview leading to existential angst).

If you think this sounds like grief, you're right. We will examine grief more closely in the next module.

RESOURCES

You are not the first person to Divorce Religion – and you won't be the last. Many others have done so in the face of daunting circumstances. Here are some videos about others who have left. *Refer to Module 1 Resources for links to the videos and articles below.*

- People who left the Amish community
- Why I left an Evangelical cult
- Leaving the Jehovah's Witnesses
- Ex-Muslim Yasmine Mohammed Speaks Out
- Why I had to leave my Ultra-Orthodox Family

We can gain insight and courage from learning about others who faced similar situations. Here are some additional documentaries that you can view on various streaming services and TV channels about insular religious groups, cults, and religious trauma:

- Bikram: Yogi, Guru, Predator (Netflix)
- Cults and Extreme Beliefs (AETV.com)
- Desperately Seeking Soulmate: Escaping Twin Flames Universe (Netflix)
- Going Clear: Scientology and the Prison of Belief (HBO, Apple, Hulu)
- Heaven's Gate: The Cult of Cults (HBO Max, Apple)
- Holy Hell (Apple TV, Prime)
- In the Name of God: A Holy Betrayal (Netflix)
- Jesus Camp (Prime, Apple TV)
- John of God: The Crimes of a Spiritual Healer (Netflix)
- Jonestown: Paradise Lost (Apple TV)
- Keep Sweet, Pray, and Obey (Netflix)
- Leah Remini: Scientology and the Aftermath (AETV.com)
- Leaving Jesus (Ellen Fiske, Momento Films)
- One of Us (Netflix)
- Prophet's Prey (Apple TV, Hulu)
- Seduced: Inside the NXIVM Cult (Crave, Hulu)
- Shiny Happy People (Apple TV, Prime)
- Sins of the Amish (Apple TV, Prime, Peacock)

- The Family (based on Jeff Sharlet's book) (Netflix)
- The Vow (HBO)
- The Way Down: God, Greed, and the Cult of Gwen Shamblin (Apple TV)
- Waco: American Apocalypse (Netflix)
- Wild, Wild Country (Netflix)

Module 1 THOUGHTFUL WORDS

Divorce is like death without a burial.
—Unattributed

*Don't ignore pain; appreciate its message:
You need to change, now!*
—Shannon L. Alder

The first revolution is when you change your mind.
—Gil Scott Heron

*Holding on is believing there is a past;
letting go is knowing there is a future.*
—Daphne Rose Kingma

You're a diamond dear. They can't break you.
—Unattributed

Module 1 Links and Resources

MODULE TWO

(Un)COMFORTABLY NUMB: Grieving Your Losses

This module encourages you to acknowledge and explore your losses, to grieve, and to grow.

When I realized that my marriage was coming to an end, I was in a state of shock. Disbelief and terror gripped me. The life I had known, for good or ill, was disappearing. A chill settled in my bones as I wondered: How did I get here? What would my life look like now? Who would I be, if not a spouse?

GRIEF

Just as marital divorce is a significant loss that induces grief and requires mourning, so it is when we Divorce Religion. The longer we have been members of a religious community, the deeper our loss.

According to JW Worden (https://whatsyourgrief.com/wordens-four-tasks-of-mourning/), four main **"tasks of mourning"** are required to complete the process of mourning and regain some sort of stability:

1. Accepting the reality of the loss.

2. Working through the pain of grief.

3. Adjusting to a new environment without the deceased (in our case, our former beliefs)

4. Withdrawing emotional energy from the deceased (our former beliefs) and reinvesting it in a new relationship. In other words, not denying our religious past, but allowing ourselves to explore and experience new thoughts, beliefs, and ways of being.

Grief is the emotional and physical response to suffering a significant loss. Mourning is our expression of that grief.

GRIEF RESPONSES

In addition to feeling sad, grief responses around losing our faith (and our related identity and community) might include feeling shocked, angry, confused, abandoned, betrayed, scared, and remorseful.

Our loss may leave us struggling with restlessness, sleep issues, weight gain or loss, forgetfulness, and trouble paying attention. Our thinking may seem slower, and we may even struggle with determining what is reality. Chest pain, digestive issues, headaches, uncontrollable crying, deep and frequent sighing, and throat tightness can also be manifestations of grief.

Just as we experience religion through the lens of our individual perception (due to experiences and personality), how we experience and express grief can also be highly individual.

Some losses are easy to see and are well recognized by society, such as the loss of loved ones, loss of our physical health, or loss of significant material possessions (e.g., in a fire). Society generally accommodates such losses, at least to some extent, acknowledging our need to mourn.

Other losses still hurt, but we are expected to bounce back from them more quickly, such as losing a job, a pet, or a shorter relationship.

However, *grief cannot be rushed*. There is no way around it; the only way out is through.

TYPES OF GRIEF AND LOSS

Did you know that there are different types of grief? Here are some that may affect us when we are Divorcing Religion:

1. **Anticipatory grief** is the distress one feels upon recognizing an impending loss, such as when we move from a fundamentalist faith to a more progressive one – only to realize that even our progressive faith is no longer sustainable. Anticipatory grief may also be present when we fear that still-religious family and friends may terminate their relationship with us upon learning of our non-belief.

2. **Ambiguous Loss** occurs when there is no closure for the bereaved. Physically, this may happen when there is no body, due to a plane crash, explosion, kidnapping, etc. **In our case, it is the loss of our faith; the dissolution of our entire worldview.** Due to its nature, ambiguous loss is particularly hard to grieve.

3. **Disenfranchised Grief** occurs over losses that are not openly acknowledged, socially sanctioned, or publicly mourned. Examples of such losses include loss by suicide, rape, abortion, a loved one going to jail for a violent crime, or the death of an extramarital affair partner. While these losses are deeply felt they are not publicly mourned, mostly due to social sanctions. **Because disenfranchised grief is relative and subjective, society at large cannot relate to it.**

4. **Unresolved grief** is grief that may last longer than usual grief. It tends to be cumulative, so every new loss adds to or re-opens it. Unresolved grief is like unfinished business.

What losses have you suffered in your life, apart from religion?

_____

_____

_____

_____

_____

Unresolved grief is more likely to occur when the bereaved:

- Is unsure how they feel about the person (in our case, the belief) that they lost
- Has a negative opinion of themselves (low self-esteem)
- Feels guilty about the loss
- Experiences the loss unexpectedly (people who experience a traumatic loss are at higher risk for developing PTSD)
- Thinks the loss was a result of unfairness (such as being deceived by a belief system)
- Experiences a loss that *others might not recognize as significant* (such as religious faith and accompanying worldview)

Unresolved grief can manifest itself in various ways, including:

- Acting like nothing has changed and refusing to discuss the loss.
- Preoccupation with the loss.

- Preoccupation with work or hobbies.
- Self-medication by way of abusing alcohol, drugs, or medicines.
- Becoming a hypochondriac (or in our case, becoming sidetracked with concern about other beliefs that we hold, chronically questioning our ability to discern fact from fiction).
- Isolating from other people and slipping into depression.
- Risky behaviors, such as stealing, gambling, and casual sex.

More information about unresolved grief can be found under Module 2 Resources.

LOSS

Divorcing Religion results in profound grief because we suffer multiple losses. This is a double whammy: First, we suffer losses as a result of embracing religion; second, we suffer additional losses as a result of divorcing it.

WHAT WE LOSE TO RELIGION:

- Acceptance of reality
- Curiosity
- Freedom
- Identity
- Individual purpose
- Pleasure
- Relationships
- Resources: Time, money, energy
- Unfettered ability to learn and grow

If raised in a fundamentalist home, we also lose the *playfulness* of childhood, becoming serious at an early age. This can affect us throughout the rest of our lives if we do not make concerted efforts to reclaim the child inside of us.

To that end, I am grateful to Hadiah for their permission to share some fantastic **worksheets to help heal your inner child.** *See Module 2 Resources for the link.*

WHAT WE LOSE WHEN WE LEAVE RELIGION:

- Assumptive worldview/order.
- Comfort and security of being on "the right" side.
- Community: Social, emotional, and sometimes financial support
- Cosmic big brother, father, lover, and whatever other relationship you were trained to believe existed between you and God.
- Face (especially if we have proselytized others and/or invested a lot of time, money, and energy in our religion).
- Feeling protected.
- Hope in a fantasy of justice and life after death.
- Sense of a higher purpose, guidance, and direction.
- Trust in others and self.

Make a list of the losses you have experienced related to leaving your religion (Community, support, worship, purpose, childcare, etc.). While this is a painful exercise, it is also very important: *We cannot grieve what we do not acknowledge.*

_____

_____

_____

_____

_____

While painful, loss is a vital step on the road to transition and transformation. The good news about loss is that it requires us to rediscover our authentic selves. *It is a poignant reality that with every loss, freedom is gained.* This freedom comes through mindfully processing our losses, as you are doing in this workbook.

Simply thinking about your losses does not get your emotional energy moving, which is why I want you to talk about them and write about them, as well as research other potentially liberating exercises. Do not remain a prisoner to your losses.

Make a list of *gains* to coincide with each of the losses listed above (This relates to *Reframing*, which we will cover more fully in a later module)

WHAT I **GAINED** WHEN I LEFT RELIGION

- Gain from losing religious rules: Autonomy
- Gain from no longer attending services: Free time
- Gain from no longer being forced to tithe: Money to save or spend
- Gain from losing religious friends: I get to choose my own, with no agenda.

- Gain from losing the support of religious family members: I get to see who has remained supportive of me and to have the opportunity to support myself.

- Gain from not having to pray: Learning to trust my intuition and my ability to make decisions

_____

_____

_____

_____

_____

Thanks to author Elizabeth Kubler Ross's book On Death and Dying (1969 Simon & Schuster), the typical emotional phases we think of related to grief include denial, anger, bargaining, depression, and acceptance – though they do not necessarily occur in this order. It is common for mourners to bounce back and forth between them and to struggle with more than one at a time.

Both bargaining and denial are a means of trying to reduce our emotional pain. While these are relatively normal coping responses, they are not sustainable in the long run.

Grief must be felt, experienced, and allowed. The deep channels carved by grief change us. Even years after our loss, we can experience unexpected "grief bursts" when something triggers us, reminding us of what we lost. This is normal – and is simply a testament to the depth of your loss. Feel it, acknowledge it, and keep living.

DEALING WITH TRIGGERS

We know we have been triggered when we experience an emotional and physiological response disproportionate to the current event. Something has occurred (we heard a song, smelled incense, drank communion-like grape juice) that has temporarily transported us back in time and threatens to overwhelm us in the present.

Physiological responses to being triggered (e.g., feeling nauseated when I drive by my old church) remind us that we have truly suffered trauma. Here are some steps for relief:

- **Remind yourself** that you are flashing back to a memory from another time, and it will pass.
- **Reassure yourself** that you are an adult now, no longer in danger, with skills and helpers available.
- **Remove yourself** if your boundaries are being violated.
- **Recall the name** of the emotion that you're feeling. This act of cognition can provide emotional space from the pain of the trigger.
- **Remember the last time** you felt this specific feeling to the same degree of intensity. When was the time before that?
- **Trace this feeling back to its origin**, as best you can. *In addition to validating your feelings, identifying the initial incident can help tone down your trigger response the next time.*

FEAR

One big emotion that comes up for many of us as we Divorce Religion is fear. Not just the fear of others finding out that we no longer believe, or the fear of losing our community; but the genuine fear of eternal damnation (Hell, eternal torment, separation from God and our loved ones) as punishment for our disbelief. In case no one has told you yet, **Hell is a man-made construct developed to control people by fear. There is no evidence for the existence of Hell.**

While the fear response itself serves an important purpose (protecting us from harm), some fears are irrational, dangerous, and need to be jettisoned. Fear of Hell falls into this category – and for some folks, it is very challenging to overcome. **Fundamentalist religions thrive on fear.** They implant it initially through threats of Hell or separation from god and family, then they enforce it in ways we likely aren't even aware of, such as demanding social conformity.

Fear is then reinforced through the hierarchical structure of religious groups, complete with varying degrees of punishment for breaking the rules, from excommunication to physical punishment. We not only fear eternal torture but also being kicked out of our community.

Those raised in strictly closed environments (various Mennonites, Amish, LDS groups, etc.) leave their groups taking with them no money, little education, and poor prospects for supporting themselves. For those brave enough to Divorce Islam, leaving can include the legitimate fear of a brutal death at the hands of those who remain fanatically attached to their beliefs.

HELP WITH OVERCOMING FEAR

My go-to method for smashing fear is always **research**. I read, watch videos, and speak with other people who have dealt with the same fear, including the fear of Hell.

It is imperative to scrutinize the validity of our fear. Is the fear based on fact, misinterpretation, or simply stories told by others trying to maintain control over you? In many cases, the one instilling the fear fails to recognize that they, themselves, were subjected to the ungrounded fear of others by way of indoctrination.

Is the fear serving you in some way, such as allowing you to make excuses rather than taking responsibility for your life?

Be ruthless in your examination of fear, leave no stone unturned.

INTRUSIVE RELIGIOUS THOUGHTS

Some people struggle with fear due to intrusive thoughts. *Scrupulosity* is the name given to obsessive-compulsive disorder related to intrusive religious thoughts. *Visit Module 2 Resources for additional information about living with religious OCD (scrupulosity).*

TIPS FOR HELPING TO ALLEVIATE THE FEAR OF HELL:

- Research when the concept of Hell (and the devil) first became popularized, and how those ideas have evolved to their current fantasy.
- Explore the afterlife beliefs of other religions, current and ancient.
- Realize that, while all religions claim to have some sort of "special knowledge," none of them actually do – because *every single religion was dreamed up by humans.*
- Reflect on the power of fear, and how it is necessary in most religions to gain, keep, and control converts.

RESOURCES RELATED TO OVERCOMING FEAR OF HELL
*See Module 2 Resources for links:

Videos:

- My interview with Dr. Caleb Lack about Treating Religious Fear and Anxiety
- CORT2022 session with Dr. Caleb Lack about Overcoming Fear of Hell
- How to Get Over the Fear of Hell, by Holy Koolaid
- How I Overcame a Fear of Hell | Life After Religion, by Sarah Elizabeth
- How Do I Get Over My Fear of Hell? by Team ROB Videos

Print Articles:

- What can you do, if you are afraid of Hell? by Dave (Sep. 6/16)
- How To Overcome the Fear of Going to Hell, by Graham Stoney (Nov. 8/16)

Many, many resources wait for you to explore! **Part of Divorcing Religion is taking responsibility for your own freedom.** Don't just settle for these few links; invest time and energy in freeing yourself. I promise you that you are worth the effort.

ANGER

Anger due to boundary violations

Anger is a legitimate part of grief. One important purpose of anger is to alert us that a boundary violation has occurred. Boundary violations are part and parcel of religious fundamentalism, especially when growing up in an authoritarian religious home.

Fundamentalism thrives on fear – and there is no greater fear for a parent than the loss of their child. In addition to fearing the death of a child, Christian parents fear that their child could reject their religious ideologies and potentially end up going to Hell, resulting in eternal separation between parent and child.

This overwhelming fear leads many parents to authoritarian parenting, where curiosity must be stamped out in favor of unquestioned obedience. Authoritarian parenting pits the natural inquisitiveness of children against power-wielding adults on a constant search for potential rebellion. All too frequently, this leads to abusive punishments (in the name of "discipline") that turn deadly.

Fear that my daughter was rebellious and destined for Hell caused me to seriously violate her privacy by reading her diary – as well as other authoritarian over-reactions I committed while under the influence of Christian parenting ideologies. I know of other parents who removed bedroom doors to prevent their child/teen from "sinning," essentially preventing the teen from having any privacy.

In the constant effort to live a sin-free life, Christianity becomes a sort of cult of confession where adults are encouraged to have "accountability partners" (especially common to prevent them from viewing sexually explicit materials). Additionally, religious adherents of all ages are told to confess potential sins to others: Children to parents, teens to youth pastors, and adults to small groups. Catholicism has elevated this Confession to the status of a sacrament.

Children learn that they are under constant scrutiny by parents and teachers always watching for sin. Eventually, we learn to police ourselves so that we are under perpetual, constant, invasive surveillance.

Christians do not have the right to boundaries, even in their minds: God is everywhere, all the time – and He is always watching (see Scrupulosity, earlier in this chapter).

Anger due to mind control and lack of choice

Boundary violations are not the only reason we may feel angry when Divorcing Religion. My religious trauma clients often experience incredible anger over having been duped into spending years of their lives in a religion that they no longer believe.

In addition to their time, many were robbed of the ability to choose their career path or life partner. Careers were to be ministry-oriented, and partners were to be biblically acceptable (opposite sex, same religion, not previously divorced).

Some went into debt to become pastors or missionaries or had impoverished childhoods due to fundamentalist parental beliefs around money and possessions. If raised by parents who believed Armageddon or The Rapture was precipitously close, higher education was discouraged altogether. Why waste money and time when Jesus' return was imminent?

For those assigned female at birth, as well as those who identify as members of the 2SLGBTQ+ community, anger and resentment may feel familiar because we were taught, in our patriarchal homes and religious communities, that we were *less than*. Lacking a penis meant we were not permitted to express our own opinions or make decisions for ourselves, and being cis-gendered and heterosexual were the only options available to us related to sexuality.

Some of my clients were denied necessities such as birth certificates, adequate education, and access to healthcare and medication because of fundamentalist parental beliefs.

Anger as a "bad" emotion

Unfortunately, in fundamentalist religious homes it is not usually permissible to express anger. The only emotions many of us were allowed to express were either forced happiness or sorrow. Anger was considered dangerous; a "bad" emotion that could lead to sin.

Patriarchal environments often permit only the male head of the family to vent his anger. Additionally, this means that children growing up in such homes do not have healthy models to follow when it comes to feeling and expressing anger or regulating emotions in general.

For those entrenched in religion, personal anger is considered sinful; only "righteous" anger is allowed. As a result, many learn to stuff or repress their anger.

Being robbed of the ability to choose is a sure-fire recipe for anger and resentment.

Anger can be helpful when it spurs us to make healthy changes — but it can be devastating if we remain steeped in it. Left unchecked, anger can lead to physical, emotional, and relational problems.

Ideas for dealing with anger:

Recognize it in your body. How can you tell you're getting angry? Do you clench your fists or your jaw? Does your neck feel hot and prickly? Learn to notice the signals your body is sending you for your own protection. Write down your physiological symptoms of anger here:

_____

_____

_____

- Consider *what* is creating your anger. Is it a person or a situation? Is it REALLY the current person or situation, or are they activating unfinished emotional business from your past?
- *What are you telling yourself* about the person or situation that is irritating you? Did they legitimately mean to offend you, or could you be misinterpreting?
- *Count to 10* before speaking.
- Treat yourself to some slow, *deep breaths*. Purposely *unclench* everything that is clenched.
- Run *cold water* over your wrists and forearms.
- Go for a *brisk walk*. Listen to a favorite song, podcast, or book while you do.
- Reach out to a *qualified secular therapist* for help with managing and expressing anger. A life free of constant angry feelings is possible.
- Check out **Module 2 Resources** for a helpful article on anger management and a fun sweary coloring page link.

TIPS TO HELP WITH GRIEF

Feeling grief takes courage. Mourning is the hardest work you will ever do, so insist on being gentle with yourself. **Self-compassion** is a necessary part of recovery.

- As with fear, **research** can be helpful when it comes to grief, even just to normalize and validate your own journey. *Find articles related to grief and loss in Module 2 Resources.*
- **Get help** if you need it. *This Survival Handbook is not meant to replace therapy*; it is simply a helpful adjunct to it. Seek out a qualified secular counsellor, coach, or consultant to

help you work through your grief over Divorcing Religion. In addition to working with clients **one-on-one**, I also offer group support calls. While **support groups** do not replace therapy, talking about your loss with others can be very healing. For information on individual sessions or group support calls, reach out to me directly at the email address listed in Module 2 Resources.

- You must **build a support network** for yourself. If you are in a larger community, there may be an in-person group you can attend for those who have left religion. By Divorcing Religion, we have lost our one-stop-shop for community, social interaction, rules, childcare, encouragement, guidance, and more. Outside of the church, it has been virtually impossible to replicate this model – which means you must do the work of taking responsibility to meet your own needs by building your own community. We will examine this more in *Module 6*.

- When working through grief, giving meaning to our loss can be helpful. One way to do this is by **donating** time or money to a humanist, scientific, atheist, or other non-religious organization.

These are some of my favorite humanist, atheist, science-oriented, non-religious organizations to donate to. *Their links are listed under Module 2 Resources on my website:*

- A Mighty Girl
- Black Nonbelievers
- Doctors Without Borders
- Freedom from Religion Foundation
- Humanists International

- Period - The Menstrual Movement to End Period Poverty
- Planned Parenthood
- Recovering from Religion
- Secular Student Alliance
- SPCA International

Take the time to truly **explore and acknowledge what you have lost**. It can be cathartic to **write a letter** to God outlining your disappointments and why you had to Divorce Religion. Go to a cemetery, stand in front of a religious statue, and read that letter. Or burn it. Or frame it. The point is to get your feelings out, complete with shedding some tears and whatever other manifestations of your loss need to be released. Put hammer to nail and pound out your frustration, sadness, and grief. My personal favorite: Burn your head covering or bury your holy book or any other representation of the years you spent being controlled by your former religious beliefs or group. Make a **releasing ceremony** out of it.

Conversely, **create something** to symbolize the change that has taken place in your life. Many of us devoted much time, energy, and creativity to our religion, serving on the worship team, dance team, sewing circle, or providing audiovisual help. *It is time to reclaim your creativity!* Paint, draw, compose, write, sculpt, or record. Make and hang art that encapsulates your feelings. This helps you acknowledge and process your feelings. You are not only releasing your pain, but you are also reclaiming your creativity and re-learning pleasure! Think of it as an exercise to help you embrace your newfound freedom.

RELIGIOUS TRAUMA AND EXISTENTIAL DEPRESSION

The ideas discussed in this portion of the Handbook are based on the work of psychiatrist Irvin D. Yalom in his excellent book Existential Psychotherapy (Basic Books, 1980).

In addition to the various forms of grief and mourning peculiar to Divorcing Religion, another issue to contend with is that of existential depression. While more "routine" forms of depression can leave people feeling sad, tearful, and lacking in motivation, existential depression tends to keep sufferers focused on four significant issues that we all must face:

1. Death
2. Freedom (choices)
3. Isolation (disconnection)
4. Meaninglessness (purpose).

Each of these gets triggered by leaving religion, especially if we have been devout Believers for a long time. For us, the main existential issues now look like this:

1. Death: Finality (no afterlife)
2. Freedom: Responsibility of having to develop our personal code of ethics
3. Isolation: Disconnection/loss of religious community
4. Meaninglessness: Loss of religious purpose (saving souls, glorifying God)

Indoctrinated with evangelical Christianity from birth, I struggled with an existential crisis in my 40s when I realized that I had mistakenly embraced religion as reality rather than myth – and that it had impacted every decision I'd made. I felt my "self" disintegrate as I had to face the future without my deeply comforting afterlife fantasy, religious moral authority, community, or purpose.

As an apostate, I felt disoriented and lonely, as well as terrified. I remember the first time the thought crept into my mind that, not only was Christianity a compilation of older religious mythologies – but maybe *God himself* was also fictitious.

While this thought was jarring, I didn't feel the full weight of my existential angst until I truly addressed the possibility of no spiritual afterlife.

The prospect of not being reunited with my loved ones after death shook me to my core. Formerly, my greatest fear had been that my children might reject Christianity; but that paled in comparison to the possibility that I might never see them, or any of my loved ones, again. It was easier to relinquish my God beliefs than it was to relinquish my afterlife fantasies.

HELPFUL TIPS for Climbing Out of Existential Depression:

If you are struggling with suicidal ideation, **reach out immediately**. In Canada and the USA, call **9-8-8** (the Suicide Crisis Helpline).

Consult this page for **Suicide Hotlines and Prevention Resources Around the World**:
https://www.psychologytoday.com/ca/basics/suicide/suicide-prevention-hotlines-resources-worldwide

Share your fears and feelings with a trustworthy person. A qualified secular therapist is a great place to start.

Work on staying present to help prevent rumination through practices like mindfulness, gratitude, and bodywork. My Divorcing Religion podcast guest, Britt Hartley, recommends feeling the water falling onto your skin in the shower, and thinking of how you would describe that sensation to someone who has never experienced it. Britt Hartley's book is called No Nonsense Spirituality: All the tools No faith required (SacraSage Press April 10, 2024)

Work on developing your emotional resilience and increasing your ability to handle distress over the unknown.

Start creating your own meaning. This begins with *clarifying your current values* to determine what is truly important to you, rather than what your parents or pastor deemed important.

Additional information on Values Clarification and Existential Depression can be found in Module 2 Resources.

When is mourning over? When we can think of our loss without feeling pain and we can emotionally reinvest in life, our time of grief and mourning is over. This is a welcome benchmark! However, your life post-grief will not be the same as it was before your loss; how could it be? Loss and grief change us.

Go back to your List of Losses and ascribe a "Pain Scale" number to each loss, with 1 being *very little* pain and 5 being *intense* pain. Do this for your initial pain and your current pain level. Revisit periodically to gauge your healing.

Module 2 THOUGHTFUL WORDS

You must give up the hope for a better past.
– Irvin Yalom

*Even the jerks earn some of our affection.
We can be glad they're gone, yet still mourn the good parts.*
– Shannon Hale

*It takes strength to make your way through grief,
to grab hold of life, and let it pull you forward.*
- Patti Davis

It's going to be hard but hard is not impossible.
- Unattributed

*When we accept all of ourselves, we become whole and healed.
Problems come from rejecting parts of ourselves.*
– Louise Hay

Module 2 Links and Resources

MODULE THREE

THE SEPARATION AGREEMENT:
Healthy Boundaries

This module encourages you to gain clarity on what you have left behind and what you are willing to accept in your new life.

Just as no two marriages are identical, divorces also vary. Some folks readily accept divorce, while others take longer to reach acceptance. Protracted, drawn-out divorces often prolong the suffering of everyone involved.

A separation agreement is a contract signed by both parties in contemplation of divorce, designed to settle issues and save emotional turmoil. The separation agreement starts to solidify the fact that your marriage cannot be saved. For this reason, it is a significant declaration.

A big part of separation involves setting and enforcing boundaries. I was married for about 20 years. We still loved each other, even as we separated. IT WAS HARD. But neither of us could embark on our new lives until we had laid the old to rest.

A dear friend gave me some solid advice, which I now pass along to you: **No sex with your ex!** No matter how lonely you feel, or how much you yearn for the familiarity of their touch. It only muddies the water, potentially dragging out your divorce even longer. The pain is not worth any temporary relief you may feel.

What does this mean in the realm of Divorcing Religion? You have already concluded that religious fundamentalism is not the right partner for you. You have begun the task of grieving your related losses. **Do not torment yourself by attending services that keep you bound to your former beliefs.**

Now is the time to contract for healthy behaviors, the time to discard old patterns of thought and behavior that no longer serve you; or worse, patterns that damage you and hold you prisoner.

It is time to confront and evaluate your thoughts, possibly incorporating some cognitive behavioral therapy (CBT) to develop healthy new thoughts and behaviors. CBT looks at how our thinking colors our interpretation of events, impacting our responses and behaviors. We tend to think the way we feel and feel the way we think. *Since this is the perfect time to learn new skills, you can find a link to explore CBT in Module 3 Resources.*

Separation Agreements are about gaining clarity. In the throes of grief, life seems murky. Our assumptive world, formed by years of indoctrination and experience, has dissolved and left us without any kind of framework to make sense of things.

You are in the process of rebuilding. Is there anything positive you can take with you from your former life? Great! Keep it. Build it into your new life. But ask yourself some hard questions, first: *Why do I like this aspect of my former life? Is it just a comforting remnant, or is it truly valuable?*

If possible, list 3 positive ideas or behaviors from your religious life that are worth incorporating into your new life:

_____

_____

_____

What was required of you by your former fundamentalist beliefs? Here is a brief list of my former religious community's requirements:

TIME: Not just Sunday morning and evening, but several nights per week, as well as daily time spent reading the Bible and praying, AKA "devotions."

CONFORMITY: No secular (nonreligious) shows, books, or music. No ingestion of secular information about science, evolution, or sex.

APPEARANCE: As a woman, long, uncut hair; long skirts/dresses only (no pants); no jewelry or makeup. My husband was to grow and maintain a beard. No tattoos or dyed hair.

MONEY: Weekly tithing, as well as additional monies given to support missionaries, etc. Purchasing of religious books, music, and household decor.

RELATIONSHIPS: No significant relationships with those "outside the fold," except for purposes of proselytizing (trying to win converts).

TALENTS: Singing, composing, leadership abilities, writing—all were to be used only to further God's kingdom, either to encourage followers or convert new ones. As a woman, I was permitted to teach other women and/or children, but not men.

The above list of religious expectations shaped my life. I prayed before dressing to ensure that nothing I wore would "cause a brother to stumble." I consulted God before saying yes to attending events (even coffee with a friend), trusting Him to "put a check in my spirit" if the plans were not ordained.

Since I believed that nothing was my own and all that I had was a result of God's great gift to me, I had to always use my time and energy in ways that expressed appropriate gratitude for that gift.

When it comes to crafting your *Separation Agreement* (template will follow), acknowledging the many ways religion controlled your life is the starting point.

What was required of you by your former fundamentalist beliefs?

_____

_____

_____

_____

_____

Fundamentalism is a form of mental hijacking, robbing us of our autonomy. Like a mental parasite, fundamentalism feeds off of us and changes our behavior to ensure its survival.

While more moderate versions of religion may foster some beneficial behaviors (such as meditation, charity, or compassion), rigid fundamentalism leads the host mind to interpret information in a specific way, so that the host becomes both irrational and delusional. For more on this idea, see Dr. Darrel Ray's book The God Virus: How Religion Infects Our Lives and Culture (© IPC Press 2009).

If you were in fundamentalism for a long time (over 40 years for me), your indoctrination was also a habit. You did not have to think about what to do, because your life was planned out according to church/temple/mosque functions. When you stopped attending, a gaping hole opened in your social life. Likewise, exactly what do you listen to or read if not sermons, your holy book, or articles relating to said book?

Your Separation Agreement is about reclaiming life *on your own terms*.

Contracting for healthy behaviors assumes that you recognize harmful ones. Consider:

Does the behavior rob you of autonomy, potential, or joy? If so, how?

_____

Does the behavior make you feel constrained, confined, or diminished? If so, how?

_____

Does the behavior feel inauthentic in any way? If so, how?

_____

I want you to consider not only why you have performed certain actions in the past, but why you continue to do so. *There are no Life Police.* You are allowed to drop and adopt behaviors according to your own desires.

After Divorcing Religion, I was happy to have my Sunday mornings back, but I missed socializing and singing. My evenings felt long and lonely and seemed to lack a sense of purpose. Spending time in my old church left me feeling sad and disappointed, as well as fearful that others would discover I no longer believed. In other words, attending church was no longer serving me.

As part of my Separation Agreement, I determined that I would spend Sunday mornings enjoying extra sleep or going out with non-church friends. For my evening free time, instead of Bible study, I decided to explore my local humanist group, which helped me socially and cognitively. My partner and I also enjoy attending lectures at our local college and university — especially on subjects that were formerly taboo. When I miss singing, rather than pine after church choir, I might host a karaoke night in my home or attend one with friends.

As noted in the previous module on grief, sometimes I donate my time or money (formerly known as my tithe) to a charity that my former self would have deeply disapproved of, like Planned Parenthood. I might also choose to spend it on a book about atheism or put it towards hosting the *Shameless Sexuality: Life After Purity Culture conference*. This money would formerly have gone to missionaries or the church, and I feel empowered using it for my preferred purposes now that I am free from religious indoctrination.

As fundamentalists, our lives were ordered by the rules of our holy book and our particular group. Christian fundamentalists are discouraged from trusting their own interpretations, their intuition, even their very thoughts: "Trust in the Lord with all your heart and *lean not on your own understanding...*" (Proverbs 3:5). The rules were there, big and small, black and white, to control us at all times — and breaking free can feel terrifying.

For some of us, we are experiencing for the first time that we are truly free and responsible for our own lives. It can feel overwhelming — but we must fight the urge to give in to that feeling. You are fully capable of deciding for yourself what to do in any given situation!

It is time to spread your wings and fly. Ups and downs will come, and you are equipped to handle them. Reach out for help from a trusted *secular* friend or counsellor if you feel stuck or need some encouragement.

Separation agreements are about *boundaries*. At the risk of offending those who view the term *codependency* as victim blaming, when we discuss the concept of boundaries related to recovery from religious trauma syndrome, we must also address **codependency** - a coping mechanism that is baked into Christianity and other high-demand groups.

CODEPENDENCY

Codependency has been described as "the need to be needed." It is a dysfunctional relationship dynamic where one person is reliant on the other to an unhealthy degree. Codependency often looks like one partner is over-functioning and the other under-functioning. Passive-aggressive behaviors and comments can point to the over-functioning partner's feelings of resentment in a relationship with codependent traits.

The term "codependency" arose in the 1950s in relation to Alcoholics Anonymous, to describe partners and loved ones of alcoholics who enable addictive behaviors.

It must be noted that codependency is not a clinical diagnosis or a personality disorder. Typically, there will be one person in the codependent partnership who identifies with the role of *giver*, and the other with the role of *taker*.

Questions to consider:

- Do you frequently apologize in your relationship, even if you don't think you've done anything wrong?
- Are you constantly concerned about how your partner is doing and whether they are upset with you?
- Do you often feel sorry for your partner?
- Do you do whatever your partner asks, even if you don't want to?

- Have you lost yourself in the partnership, needing constant external approval that is nearly impossible to get?

How religions prime followers for codependency

These can all point to codependency – which fundamentalist Christianity (and other religions) primes us for in the following ways:

- Discouraging boundaries.
- Encouraging constant service to others (Jesus first, others second, you last).
- Discouraging pride and healthy self-esteem.
- Discouraging expressions of anger.
- Telling us to become empty of ourselves so there is more room for Jesus.
- Implying that we are incapable of making decisions without consulting God or a pastor.

Links for these helpful articles about Codependency can be found under Module 3 Resources on my website:

- How Christianity Encourages Codependence, by KC Brown
- The Causes of Codependency, by Sun Behavioral Health
- Understanding Codependence as "Soft-Core" Cult Dynamics, from Pair A Docks
- How to Spot the Signs of Codependency, by Wendy Rose Gould

Recognizing a propensity towards codependency or emotional enmeshment is vital for us to change and become comfortable with setting and enforcing boundaries.

DIVINE/RELIGIOUS TRAUMA BONDING

Another issue that makes it difficult to clearly see reality and set appropriate boundaries is trauma bonding, which is a psychological response to abuse more likely to occur when shame or danger is present. In such situations, the person suffering the abuse may develop feelings of empathy and affection for their abuser, similar to Stockholm Syndrome. *See Module 3 Resources for more information on Trauma Bonding and Stockholm Syndrome.*

Situations with a cycle of abuse followed by apologies, promises, and positive reinforcement lend themselves to trauma bonding. The victim doubts whether the abuse is real because the abuser professes to love them.

The God of the Bible insisting that He loves Humanity deeply *but will torture us all for eternity if we reject that love* sets the basis for a potential trauma bond. The story of Noah's ark – highly glossed over as a favorite for toddlers – is a prime example of this. After killing every living thing on the planet except eight people and a boat full of animals, God declares his love for Humanity by promising never to kill them all again; or at least, not in that way.

Victims of what I call Divine trauma bonding share similarities with those bonded to domestic abusers, including making excuses for their abuser and holding misplaced loyalty which can cause fear and discomfort around the thought of leaving. Divine trauma bonding can also leave survivors feeling that the abuse was somehow their fault.

As with codependency, trauma bonding is a survival mechanism based on the need for attachment. Like victims of kidnapping who are dependent on their captors for survival, those of us programmed by Christianity feel dependent on God for our safety and survival – the same god who promises to torture us if we reject His "love."

It's easy to see how we can become trauma-bound not only to the Christian God but also to our religious community who reinforce our feelings of fear and love. Eventually, we internalize both the threats of Hell and the professions of Divine love so deeply that we police ourselves.

As with survivors of domestic abuse, those who have suffered Divine/religious trauma bonding may find it hard to break free. For those of us who manage to do so, depression, anxiety, and low self-esteem may be chronic companions. In such cases, it is wise to obtain the help of a qualified secular therapist.

SEPARATION AGREEMENT TEMPLATE

Now that you have a greater understanding of boundary infringements and how fundamentalism hijacked and controlled your life, here is a template to get you started. You are free to craft your own Separation Agreement, updating it if and whenever you choose. **It is a declaration to yourself that you are taking control of your own life, officially separating from the dogmas of religious fundamentalism.**

SEPARATION AGREEMENT FROM RELIGIOUS FUNDAMENTALISM

Dated this _____ of _____, _____

BETWEEN:

(Name) _____ and

(Name of religion) _____

BACKGROUND:

I acknowledge that I formerly partnered with

_____ (religious group) from the date of _____ to _____.

For purposes of my emotional well-being and desired personal growth, we are now separated from one another.

This is not a binding or legal contract. Rather, it serves to clarify and remind me of the many reasons I have decided to Divorce Religion and live a life of emotional and intellectual freedom.

I now invoke my right as an autonomous, adult human to break all emotional and psychological bonds associated with

_____ (religion), including the rejection of any promises or covenants I made under emotional, spiritual, or psychological duress.

As of _____ (today's date), I assume control over my own life including, but not limited to, such areas as:

How I spend my time

How I spend my money

How I dress

What I watch, read, or listen to

With whom I will associate

What I believe

FURTHERMORE:

I hereby agree to swap out the following behaviors formerly appropriated by religious fundamentalism:

THE SEPARATION AGREEMENT: HEALTHY BOUNDARIES

Instead of

Attending religious services, I will:

_____

Listening to religious music, I will listen to:

_____

Using my time and resources to expand the church, I will use my time and resources to:

_____

Reading religious literature, I will read:

_____

Use the spaces below to list any other ideas or behaviors you wish to liberate and reclaim for yourself:

_____

_____

_____

Signed:

_____

How are you feeling right now? This exercise likely evoked strong emotions and memories. I hope you found it both cathartic and clarifying. Your journey from fundamentalism to freedom is well underway. There is one last item to consider in this phase of your transition. It has roots in Module 2 (grief) and lays the framework for Module 4 (identity reconstruction):

THE VOID

We lose a lot when we Divorce Religion. Sometimes it feels like there is more of us missing than is still present. For some, the greatest loss is the sense of community; for others, it is the feeling of comfort and certainty that we had with our former beliefs. The multiple losses combined represent what I call *The Void*.

Sometimes, The Void feels lonely. Often, it feels downright terrifying. The Void is that space between *What Was* and *What Will Be*. It is the space you sometimes weep in, longing for a past that you can never return to, frightfully uncertain of your future. It is the space you sometimes dream in, peering into the mist, longing to see your new world take shape.

Though painful, The Void is a powerful space. It is fertile ground. The old you has died, and it is within the sacred (let's reclaim this word) space of The Void that your new self is being created.

Embrace The Void as a gift. For some, this is your first time having the freedom to think independent thoughts, to explore and research anything of interest. It is a time of creation; your old self has been shed and your new self is beginning to exist. While others also experience their own Void during the transition, yours is unique. Some solitude can be beneficial during this time, as you allow yourself to contemplate Becoming.

Module 3 THOUGHTFUL WORDS

*You can't change someone who does not
see an issue with their actions.*
—Unattributed

Choose to be a student of life rather than a victim of circumstance.
—Unattributed

The flower that blooms from destruction is called FREEDOM.
—Unattributed

"The price of anything is the amount of life you exchange for it."
—H.D. Thoreau

Nature abhors a vacuum.
—Aristotle

Module 3 Links and Resources

I found Dr. Bobby Azarian's article *How Religious Fundamentalism Hijacks the Brain* to be very interesting. The link is under Module 3 Resources on my website, with the other resources mentioned.

MODULE FOUR

Getting Along with Yourself and Your Ex

Part A: IDENTITY RECONSTRUCTION

This part is designed to move you from spiritual refugee to bold adventurer.

My former identity was as a fundamentalist Christian wife, stay-at-home mother (SAHM), and homeschooler. My decisions and identity reflected my beliefs about the Bible as the literal and inspired word of God. Unfortunately, as my beliefs dissolved, so did my identity.

When I had to join the workforce to help support our family, it chipped away at my pride over being a SAHM. I truly believed that a woman's place was in the home. It also meant I had to give up homeschooling, which had been another essential aspect of my fundamentalist identity.

Both losses reflect how **my beliefs and identity had become enmeshed**. The end of my marriage was another huge blow to the identity I had erected. I cried when I renewed my driver's license and resumed using my maiden name. *Who was I now*, if not even a wife? My religious, cultural, and familial beliefs around marriage and divorce threatened to crush me in my grief.

My last familiar and comforting shred of identity was my belief that Jesus still loved me. Eventually, even that aspect of my identity dissolved – and I stepped into The Void mentioned at the end of Module 3.

For a long while, I alternated between feelings of numbness, shock, fear, and disbelief. My entire life, along with my entire assumptive worldview, had disintegrated. The floor beneath me seemed to disappear and I was in a free fall. No longer a wife. No longer a SAHM. No longer a member of any church, Bible study, or women's group. In fact, I was no longer even a Christian, after nearly four decades spent in that club.

What helped me start putting my own pieces back together? Reading. For the first time in my life, I gave myself permission to read anything that I wanted. *Nothing* would be off-limits to me ever again. Astrology? Other religions? Evolutionary texts? The Kama Sutra? YES! I permitted myself to explore, without limits.

The trauma of losing my faith split me open – and books on every topic, from every perspective, planted seeds that helped me grow. I eventually recognized the tremendous potential found in The Void, especially for rebuilding my identity. For the first time in my life, I was free from the smothering cloak of expectations placed on me by others.

Investigation. Exploration. Experimentation. These are all words that describe the Identity Reconstruction phase of our Divorce. This can be a joyful and empowering time and one that ought not to be rushed. Courage and contemplation are helpful allies in The Void.

Explore everything that interests you by way of books, videos, websites, podcasts, courses, and more. Attend live events like music festivals, art galleries, and science exhibits. Anything that piques your interest is worthy of investigation. For years, you likely had serious restrictions placed upon your intellect and curiosity. All information was sifted through your religious lens of perception and quickly discarded if it challenged your belief system.

Your *Separation Agreement* from Module 3 may help point you in the direction of formerly forbidden fruit, which often makes the tastiest jam!

"It is noble to suffer; suffering will be rewarded" is a cosmic mythology well-rooted in Christianity. Many of us have had to defy our parents and teachers simply to enjoy normal activities such as attending movies or sporting events.

One friend recounted the time her religious school principal found out students were attending the local roller rink – so he made his way to the middle of that rink, knelt, and prayed aloud for their salvation. Talk about a downer. Such baggage can make it difficult for us to relax and have a good time once we have Divorced Religion. *We have been taught that having fun and enjoying life outside of religion is sinful.*

It takes courage to investigate ideas and actions that you were taught were sinful or dangerous. You may need to write yourself a *permission slip* that you keep somewhere visible to remind you that YOU ARE NOW FREE. I still have mine, written on an old recipe card that is now faded and worn.

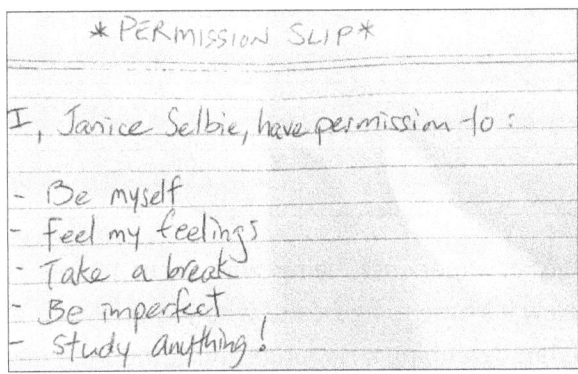

My old permission slip

It says:

PERMISSION SLIP

I, Janice Selbie, have permission to:

- Be Myself
- Feel my feelings
- Take a break
- Be imperfect
- Study anything!

Reflecting on what religion simultaneously imposed on you and denied you, what do you need to give yourself permission to do?

PERMISSION SLIP

I, _____, have permission to:

_____

_____

_____

_____

_____

_____

You have lots of experience being who other people thought you should be. Now it's time to figure out who you really are, and who you want to be. Start by gaining knowledge and gathering experiences. Ask questions. Take notes. Enjoy your freedom.

You do not need to feel hemmed in, guilty, or ashamed. *Shame is part of fundamentalism, not of freedom.* Some of us need to actively liberate ourselves by doing something formerly forbidden to us like:

- Visiting a winery
- Swearing out loud
- Making a naughty cross-stitch
- Masturbating
- Writing a dirty limerick, or something else that symbolizes our freedom.

Remember: If it is not breaking the law or harming another person, you are free to do it!

Fundamentalists are cursed with responsibility and seriousness from an early age. Our natural curiosity and desire to explore was either snuffed out completely or directed only to *appropriate* religious/spiritual outlets. Creativity was viewed as a gift from God, for God. Nonsense! You belong to yourself, as do your thoughts, abilities, desires, and creativity.

Some of my abilities that were held hostage to religion included writing, music, acting, and leadership.

Take some time to consider how your natural abilities and curiosities were affected:

_____

_____

_____

_____

Here are some of the things I explored during my Identity Reconstruction: New age philosophies, Buddhism, Hinduism, crystals, chakras, and sex. I taught myself to meditate, grew dreadlocks, and got tattoos. I enjoyed some romantic liaisons that would have previously been off-limits to me, joined a rock band, and even tried my hand at comedy (Google *Georgie & Glo* for proof). I acquainted myself with Richard Dawkins and other famous atheists whom I had previously prayed for (and against). *For an interesting list of Famous Atheists and Agnostics, compiled by CBS News, see Module 4 Resources on my website.*

CAVEAT

There is one caveat to consider during your Identity Reconstruction which we will explore in detail in Module 7: The danger of falling prey to other dogmatic views and groups.

At some point in fundamentalism, you became comfortable with binary, all-or-nothing thinking; with rules and regulations that, while making you feel safe, prevented you from accepting information from those outside your religious group. A precedent has been set, a comfort zone of sorts.

Divorcing Religion is hard work. It's much easier having someone else tell you what the rules are. If you were indoctrinated most of your life, making decisions on your own can feel threatening and overwhelming — leaving you vulnerable to adopting other, equally dogmatic views.

Do not be in such a rush to fill The Void that you latch onto another equally dogmatic and isolating identity. Research. Experiment. Bite off tiny pieces to see how they taste. If you try something and it doesn't sit well with you, spit it out — and move on to your next course!

This is a time of liberty in your life. Feel free to accept and reject new ideas, experiences, and philosophies. Your choices are not carved in stone. You are allowed to grow and change, and your needs and desires can change, too.

List some philosophies or activities that you are curious about:

_____

_____

_____

_____

At this point, it may be helpful to think of yourself less as a spiritual refugee and more as a sojourner, an explorer on a spiritual or philosophical safari. Open yourself up to new thoughts and experiences. Even if you don't find anything that suits you, you will end up with some interesting memories from your trip!

Some Divorce Religion and decide to take up with a similar but more liberal partner such as new age mysticism, Buddhism, or Wicca. Others make their way to humanism, agnosticism, and atheism, feeling more comfortable in the realm of science than traditional spirituality.

I also appreciate the philosophy of naturalism, which is a way of understanding the world based on science. It asserts that everything that exists, no matter how complex, is part of the natural world, and there is no separate supernatural or magical realm. *See Module 4 Resources for more information on Naturalism.*

This is YOUR journey. You are the driver and the passenger, determining where you travel and how long you stay, as well as what souvenirs you choose to keep. The goal here is to expand your mind and your life experience. While this is sometimes painful, it is always valuable.

Module 4A THOUGHTFUL WORDS

This is the part where you find out who you are.
—Unattributed

"When I discover who I am, I'll be free."
—Ralph Ellison, Invisible Man

An identity would seem to be arrived at by the way the person faces and uses [their] experience.
—James Baldwin

"I said to the sun, 'Tell me about the Big Bang.' The sun said, 'It hurts to become.'"
—Andrea Gibson

"I am no bird, and no net ensnares me: I am a free human being with an independent will."
—Charlotte Brontë, Jane Eyre

Part B: PURITY CULTURE RECOVERY

Welcome to Shameless Sexuality: Life After Purity Culture

Exploring identity includes exploring our *sexual* identity. If your family practiced one of the Abrahamic religions, there is a good chance you were impacted by dysfunctional teachings about your body and sex. Simply by growing up in Canada or the USA – without even being raised in a religious home – it's likely that extremely conservative attitudes about sex affected your life. In Evangelical circles, the obsession with virginity and forced abstinence, including the attempted control of the bodies of girls and women and the minds of boys and men, is commonly referred to as *Purity Culture*.

Growing up in an Evangelical home, the concept of virginity caused me great distress. Like millions of other children raised by religious parents, I was sadly misinformed and brainwashed to believe that NOTHING was more important than me, as a woman, being "a virgin" on my wedding night.

Imagine my surprise when I learned (in my 40s) that the whole concept of virginity is merely a social construct! Why? Because *virginity is not a natural or objective fact, but a cultural and historical idea that varies across time and place.*

Put simply: Virginity is a concept that people use to define, regulate, and judge sexual behavior and morality, often *with different standards and expectations for different genders.*

Virginity is not based on any scientific or biological evidence, but on myths, beliefs, and norms that can be harmful, oppressive, and discriminatory.

Take the time to review these helpful, and maybe surprising, articles about virginity. *Links available in Module 4 Resources on my website*

- Why Virginity is a Social Construct, from the Hana website
- Virginity is a Social Construct, But What Does That Mean? by Kristin Mae
- Virginity is A Social Construct, on the Therapy for Women website

Content Warning: Things are about to get graphic...

There is no clear or universal definition of what virginity is or how it is "lost." Different people may have different understandings of what counts as sex, and what changes - or does not change - after having sex.

For example, some people may consider oral or anal sex as sex, while others may not. Some people may consider masturbation or using sex toys as "losing virginity," while others may not. Some people may consider virginity as a state of mind, while others may not.

There is no reliable or consistent way to test or prove virginity. The most common myth is that the hymen, a thin membrane that partially covers the vaginal opening, is a sign of virginity that breaks or bleeds during the first intercourse. *However, this is not true*, as the hymen can vary in shape, size, and elasticity, and can be stretched or torn by other activities besides sex.

Moreover, not all girls have a hymen, and not all of us bleed or feel pain during our first intercourse. Therefore, **the hymen is not a valid indicator of virginity, and neither is blood or pain.**

There is no inherent or intrinsic value or meaning attached to virginity. The value or meaning of virginity is determined by social and cultural factors, such as religion, morality, tradition, law, politics, economics, or media.

Different societies and communities may have different views and norms about virginity and may reward or punish people according to those views. For example, some cultures mistakenly value virginity as a symbol of purity, honor, or fidelity. These cultures may require or expect people, *especially uterus owners*, to "remain virgins" (i.e., abstain from penis-in-vagina sex) until marriage.

Other groups may view virginity as a sign of ignorance, immaturity, or weakness, and may encourage or pressure people, *especially penis owners*, to become sexually active as soon as possible. These views and norms can affect how people feel about themselves and their sexuality, and how they are treated by others.

"Honour-based" Violence

Horrifically, some patrilineal religious groups and cultures believe it is acceptable for families to murder female family members who are suspected of premarital sex, adultery, or disobedience. Very inaccurately, such murders are referred to as *honor killings*. Honour-based violence is religious trauma of the highest order, and there should be no place for it in the 21st Century.

According to Sharif Kanaana, professor of anthropology at Birzeit University:

"What the men of the family, clan, or tribe seek control of in a patrilineal society is reproductive power. Women for the tribe were considered a factory for making men." Ruggi, S., "Commodifying Honor in Female Sexuality: Honor Killings in Palestine". Middle East Research and Information Project. http://www.merip.org/mer/mer206/ruggi.htm. Retrieved 2008-02-08.

Since there is no honour in killing, I shall refer to these acts as murders.[7] While the majority of such murders occur within Muslim communities, they also occur in the north of India. Sadly, they also happen in North America. The following two heart-breaking examples occurred in Canada. Unfortunately, I had a large number of similar cases to choose from.

Links available in Module 4 Resources.

---

[7] https://www.theguardian.com/commentisfree/2014/jun/23/stop-honour-killing-murder-women-oppresive-patriarchy

On New Year's Day of 2009, 22-year-old Amandeep Kaur Dhillon was stabbed to death by her father-in-law. He told police he was justified in killing her because she was about to dishonor their family by leaving their son for another man.[8]

In June 2010, 16-year-old Aqsa Parvez was murdered by her father and her brother, who strangled her to death. According to her friends, Aqsa's refusal to wear the hijab (Islamic headscarf) was creating conflict in her family.[9]

THE BIBLE AND SEX

Here are just a few of the many harmful teachings from the Bible around sex and sexuality that contribute to toxic Purity Culture indoctrination:

Sex is only for procreation and not for pleasure or intimacy.

This view ignores the emotional, relational, and spiritual aspects of sex, and reduces it to a biological function. It also denies the value and dignity of people who are infertile, celibate, or sexually inactive.

Sex is dirty, shameful, or defiling.

This view creates a negative attitude towards sex and one's own body and fosters guilt, fear, and repression.

Sex is only for heterosexual marriage and any other form of sex is unnatural or perverse.

This view excludes and stigmatizes people who are single, divorced, widowed, or LGBTQ+, and denies them the possibility of love, intimacy,

---

[8] https://www.justice.gc.ca/eng/rp-pr/cj-jp/fv-vf/hk-ch/p2.html
[9] https://www.thestar.com/news/crime/i-killed-my-daughter-with-my-hands/article_cec7714d-78fd-5212-a430-1b3dc7de47ec.html

and fulfillment. It also ignores the diversity and complexity of human sexuality and gender identity, and the reality of sexual abuse, violence, and exploitation.

Sex is a matter of male authority and female submission.

This view reinforces patriarchal and sexist norms that oppress and exploit women and limit their agency, autonomy, and equality - not to mention, their right to experience pleasure.

IS PORNOGRAPHY TRULY BAD?

If your first thought is *"Ix-nay on the orn-pay,"* please keep reading. As long as humans have had the capacity to draw and create, there have been depictions of humans engaging in sexual activity (see *Ain Sakhri figurine* for the oldest known representation of humans having sex).

Humans are curious about their own bodies and the bodies of others, and we LOVE pleasure in pretty much every way possible. There is no shame in this fact about humanity. Pornography gets a bad rap, mainly from those carrying religious shame around sex and nudity. However, we do live in an age where sex trafficking is a sad reality, and it is sometimes filmed and marketed as porn.

How can we be sure our viewing habits align with our values such that we do not contribute to the sexual exploitation of others? By only viewing *ethical* porn. Ethical porn means all actors involved are of legal adult age; they are there because they want to participate; and they fully consent to the film being made. Additionally, safety precautions are taken by those involved, and there is fair compensation for the actors. Ethical porn can be inclusive and empowering, as well as varied and spicy.

*See Module 4 Resources, at the end of this module, for a list of ethical porn sites.

MONOGAMISH

When I was in primary school, my parents splurged on a new dining room set and I was excited to share about it during show and tell. My teacher smiled at my answer when she asked what type of wood the new furniture was made from, and I innocently replied, "I think it's monogamy." She gently responded that it was probably *mahogany* (we were both wrong; it was teak).

Many who marry young, due to the religious pressure not to have sex outside of marriage, marry a partner they would not have married otherwise. The most important thing about marriage in a fundamentalist community is that one marries within that community, abiding by the prescribed norms of a male marrying a female.

Some people who experience religious deconversion also recognize that they are no longer satisfied in a monogamous relationship with the person they married under religious pressure. Divorce is not the only option. Some couples, who want to maintain their partnership but explore other options, move towards ethical nonmonogamy.

I found the article *What is Ethical Nonmonogamy? An Intro to ENM Relationships*, on the Attachment Project website, helpful to understand this topic. I also appreciated the piece *11 Fundamental Forms of Ethical Nonmonogamy, Explained*, by Sophie Saint Thomas. *Links for both are in the Module 4 Resources.*

Opening one's relationship is not for the faint-hearted. While it may feel tempting to jump into swinging or similar activities, such changes are not to be undertaken without significant research, discussion, and potential relationship counselling. In the Memoir portion of this book, I mentioned that being in an open relationship with Luke did not work for me. However, I do know couples for whom it genuinely does work.

Here are some popular books on the topic:

The Ethical Slut (Hardy, Janet W. and Easton, Dossie. *The Ethical Slut: A Guide to Infinite Sexual Possibilities.* Greenery Press. 1997)

Polysecure (Fern, Jessica. Polysecure: Attachment, Trauma, and Consensual Nonmonogamy. Thornapple Press. 2020)

Opening Up (Taormino, Tristan. Opening Up: A Guide to Creating and Sustaining Open Relationships. Cleis Press. 2008)

More Than Two (Veaux, Franklin and Rickert, Eve. *More Than Two: A Practical Guide to Ethical Polyamory* Thorntree Press. 2014)

The Jealousy Workbook (Labriola, Kathy. *The Jealousy Workbook: Exercises and Insights for Managing Open Relationships.* Greenery Press. 2013)

Growing up in a fundamentalist home, we were denied the freedom to explore ourselves sexually and even to explore our own gender identity. We were categorized according to genitalia and expected to abide by binary male and female gender roles and norms, only.

TROUBLE THINKING STRAIGHT?

While I recognized my attraction to boys and girls during childhood and adolescence, I did not feel free to explore my sexuality until I was in my 40s. The joy and fulfillment I experienced in dating other women laid to rest my need to pretend I was anything other than bisexual. I could finally be comfortable in my own sexual skin.

In addition to religious trauma survivors questioning whether they want to stay married to a person they married under religious pressure (rather than sincere attraction), some people also question their gender identity, attraction, and expression. Here are some terms that may be helpful as you explore sexuality:

Gender Identity: This is how a person feels inside, whether they feel like a male, a female, both, neither, or something else entirely. It's who you know yourself to be, whether you feel like a man, a woman, or somewhere in between.

Gender Expression: This is how a person shows their gender to the world through clothes, hairstyles, mannerisms, or behaviors. It's about how you present yourself to others, whether it's more masculine, feminine, or a mix of both.

Biological Sex: This refers to the physical aspects of being male, female, or intersex, which are determined by chromosomes, hormones, and reproductive organs. It's about the body you were born with, whether you have male or female reproductive organs, and characteristics like genitalia, pitch of voice, body hair, etc.

For more links about terms related to identity, sex, and relationships; as well as links for the speakers listed below, see Module 4 Resources.

Here are some of the sexologists, sex therapists, and Purity Culture survivors who have been featured on the Divorcing Religion Podcast and the inaugural Shameless Sexuality: Life After Purity Culture Conference:

- Anthony Venn Brown, Founder and CEO of Ambassadors & Bridge Builders International TOPIC: A Life of Unlearning, From Gay Shame to Gay Pride
- Charone Pagett TOPIC: Purity Culture is Just Ablest - Why Purity Culture Ignores Disabled Women
- Danielle Kramer, LLC, Sex therapist and clinical sexologist TOPIC: Toxic Purity – Unpacking the Patriarchy
- David Teachout, Therapist TOPIC: The Continuing Religious Trauma of Demands for Purity

- Dr. Darrel Ray, Founder/President Recovering from Religion and The Secular Therapy Project TOPIC: The Sex Addiction Panic and Its Religious Roots

- Erica Smith, Sex Educator TOPIC: Dating and Sex After Purity Culture

- Dr. Lauren Walker, Psychologist and Researcher TOPIC: Sexual Desire and Response - Addressing Lasting Influences from Purity Culture

- Dr. Laurie Mintz, Psychologist and Certified Sex Therapist TOPIC: Orgasm Gap Causes and Solutions

- Marie LePage, Humanity Coach TOPIC: Remedial Consent Education for Former Fundamentalists

- Dr. Marlene Winell, Licensed Psychologist TOPIC: Fireside Chat

- Rebecca Williams, LMFT TOPIC: Aren't You A Little Old for That? Exploring the experience of a formerly religious Later-in-Life Lesbian

- Dr. Sara Moslener, Writer, Researcher, Lecturer TOPIC: Sexual Purity and the Construction of White Women's Racial Identity

- Steven Davidson PhD, LCSW TOPIC: Eroticism/Kink/Fetishes

Video sessions from all Shameless Sexuality speakers can be found on my YouTube channel: https://www.youtube.com/@ComeToCORT

SEXUAL VALUES EXERCISE: Create Your YES /NO / MAYBE List

It's time to consider your personal sexual values and create a *Yes/No/Maybe List* for present and future sexploration! You are allowed to change your mind - and your list - at any time.

I recommend you do this thoughtfully on your own; then, you can share it with trusted partner(s) if you like. NOTE: This information is not typically first-date material.

Your list can be basic or graphic or both. You may want to categorize your questions into Words, Body Part Boundaries, Relationship Types, Actions, etc. When it comes to Actions, use Y for Yes, N for No, M for Maybe, and U for Unsure.

Here are some questions to help get you started:

How do you view your sexual orientation or identity?

_____

Are you comfortable with others knowing this about you? Y/N/M/U

_____

How do you feel about sexting with words or photos? Y/N/M/U

_____

Do you like or dislike sexy talking during sex? Y/N/M/U

_____

Do you like or dislike public displays of affection? Y/N/M/U

_____

Do you prefer lights on or off during times of sexual intimacy?

___

Are you open to using sex toys, either solo or with partners? Y/N/M/U

___

How do you feel about discussing intimate sexual details with others who were not there? Y/N/M/U

___

What words do you prefer for your genitals?

___

Do you like being:

Caressed? Y/N/M/U If so, where?

___

Licked? Y/N/M/U

If so, where?

___

Pinched? Y/N/M/U If so, where?

___

Restrained? Y/N/M/U (see Module 4 Resources to learn more)

If so, do you prefer having your hands or your legs restrained, or both?

___

What type of restraints?

_____

Tickled? Y/N/M/U If so, tickled with what?

_____

Are you open to ethical non-monogamy, swinging, or polyamory? Y/N/M/U

_____

Are you comfortable with viewing porn either alone or solo? Y/N/M/U

_____

If so, what type(s) are exciting to you?

_____

Are you open to role-playing? Y/N/M/U
If yes, what scenarios are appealing to you?

_____

_____

_____

_____

Are any parts of your body off-limits to partners? If so, which ones?

_____

_____

_____

_____

See the *Module 4 Resources on my website* for Simon Fraser University's terrific Yes/No/Maybe Checklist page with links to additional lists to help you communicate about sex, physical intimacy, consent, and fun between sexual partners. Under *Module 4 Resources*, you'll also find additional links to juicy articles and sites about:

- Ethical porn
- Identity, sex, and relationships
- Sex therapist training

Module 4B Thoughtful words:

This is the part where you find out who you are.
— Unattributed

Sex is a part of nature. I go along with nature.
—Marilyn Monroe

Sex is emotion in motion.
—Mae West

Sex appeal is not in your body parts. It's in you.
—Neha Bhasi

There is no age limit on the enjoyment of sex. It keeps getting better.
—Florence Henderson

> *In America, sex is an obsession.*
> *In other parts of the world, it's a fact.*
> —Marlene Dietrich

Now that we've covered some significant issues related to identity, we can start to consider what sort of *life philosophy* fits us in our current state.

Part C: LIFE PHILOSOPHY

If you were a Christian, you were likely familiar with the Apostle's Creed or the Nicene Creed. Muslims have their creed, known as The Shahada. While these are religious, a creed can be loosely defined as a system or formula of belief. In this part of the module, you will consider your personal creed, of sorts: your Life Philosophy.

If indoctrinated in childhood, your beliefs about yourself and the world around you were hijacked by religion. Natural curiosity was replaced with rules of obedience in thought and deed. You were likely also indoctrinated to believe that there was nothing good about you, nothing for you to be proud of.

Pride itself (which is the natural result of mastering a task we have worked at) was probably considered a sin. During this time of Identity Reconstruction, it's time to review your existing skills, abilities, and desires — and determine what else you would like to add to your magnificent self!

In religious communities, we are chided for being vain if we show any pride in our abilities. Instead, we are taught that nothing good comes from us; good only comes from God working in or through us.

This is extremely disempowering, training us to be utterly dependent upon God (an *outside* source) and to shirk our responsibility for developing life skills. This unnatural state often leaves us developmentally lagging behind our secular peers, and it requires dedication and courage to overcome.

Maturity requires you to **recognize your strengths** and use them to help build your new life. If you have trouble doing so, ask a trusted friend what they see as some of your strengths.

INVENTORY OF STRENGTHS

Start by listing 20 things you like about yourself. These can include character traits, skills, and accomplishments:

1. _____

2. _____

3. _____

4. _____

5. _____

6. _____

7. _____

8. _____

9. _____

GETTING ALONG WITH YOURSELF AND YOUR EX

10. _____

11. _____

12. _____

13. _____

14. _____

15. _____

16. _____

17. _____

18. _____

19. _____

20. _____

Some folks find that a challenging assignment, which makes it all the more valuable. I hope that you will save this list and add to it in the days and years to come.

VALUES VISION QUEST

You are now without a religious framework to guide your morality. While I am certain that you are fully capable of acting decently towards others without a religion guiding you, it is natural to seek out both a philosophy and a community that reflects your values.

For those of us who grew up in rigid, authoritarian communities it can be a challenge to determine our personal values apart from those that were imposed on us by parents or group leaders. This is where Values Clarification work can be a fantastic tool.

Values clarification is figuring out what matters to you. Clarifying our values helps guide us in our daily activities, allowing us to stay true to ourselves. Once you determine which values are your most important, you can see whether your career, relationships, and resource expenditure are in alignment with those values.

As a devout Believer, my highest values were obedience, submission, and holiness. Now, they are autonomy, freedom, and curiosity. Knowing this about myself has helped me recognize when codependency is at play. Remembering my values, I now only participate in activities when I truly want to – instead of when I feel obligated to do so, out of fear of disappointing others.

Atheists are often accused of having no morals, since religious folk believe that morality needs to come from an outside authority. In fact, there is some evidence that humans have developed innate morality by way of evolution. Check out Greg Epstein's book *Good Without God: What a Billion People Do Believe* (William Morrow 2009), and books by sociologist Phil Zuckerman on the topic of secular morality. *See Module 4 Resources*

Though I used to fear "Secular Humanist" values, now I know that they emphasize the importance of compassion, empathy, reason, and critical thinking in guiding behavior. Humanists prioritize the well-being and dignity of all individuals, promoting equality, justice, and human rights. Humanist values also emphasize the importance of personal autonomy, freedom of thought, and ethical decision-making based on rationality and evidence. Overall, humanist values emphasize the potential for human beings to lead fulfilling and meaningful lives through fostering positive relationships, contributing to the greater good, and pursuing knowledge and understanding.

See Module 4 Resources for links about Humanism, including the poster mentioned below and the UN Declaration of Human Rights.

Far superior to the Ten Commandments, The American Humanist Center for Education developed the **10 Humanist Commitments**, which include:

1. Altruism
2. Critical Thinking
3. Empathy
4. Environmentalism
5. Ethical Development
6. Global Awareness
7. Humility
8. Peace and Social Justice
9. Responsibility
10. Service and Participation.

DOCTRINE DETOX

In order to reconstruct, deconstruction must first take place. An exercise I've found helpful is to **consider what you were taught in your religion and contrast it with what you believe now**. You may have avoided this task previously, as it can be humbling and shocking to closely examine what we once believed wholeheartedly. This is where your *Separation Agreement* from the previous module may prove helpful, at least to get you started.

Here are some of my own contrasting views, as an example:

*MY **FORMER** VIEWS ABOUT:*

Myself – I was useless and worthless apart from being a vessel for God to bring others into His Kingdom either through proselytizing or giving birth

Other people – They were broken, desperate, and wicked sinners

Other religions – All were cults; deceived, depraved, Hell-bound

The world – An evil, dark place; the dominion of Satan; unsafe; destined for demolition

The future – No hope apart from God and (my brand of) Christianity. All outside my religion would spend eternity in Hell.

Love – Love is a gift from God, an example of His love for us. Love for my spouse should cover or make allowance for their imperfections – even neglect or abuse.

Sex – Outside of heterosexual marriage sex is deviant, sinful, and unacceptable.

*MY **CURRENT** VIEWS ABOUT:*

Myself – I am unique and complicated, with a clever mind and compassionate spirit

Other people – Each person has value and can teach me something

Other religions – Religions originally developed as stories to explain natural events and are often used to control people

The world – Is a beautiful place, filled with incredible sights, people, and lessons!

The future – Is my own to map out and create. The choices I make today can influence my future. I am powerful!

Love – The feeling of love is a result of attachment to another being. Loving myself means I do not tolerate abusive behavior.

Sex – Sex is physiologically and emotionally beneficial. It is always to be pleasurable. While sex must only be between consenting adults, the gender(s) of those involved has no bearing on morality. Sex is natural and fun!

Now I invite you to craft your list of current and former views.

*MY **FORMER** VIEWS ABOUT:*

_____

_____

_____

_____

_____

MY **CURRENT** VIEWS ABOUT:

_____
_____
_____
_____
_____
_____
_____

It is especially valuable to examine beliefs that inform the way you see and treat yourself and others. Questions to ask include:

What is my belief about?

_____

When did I develop that belief?

_____

Who introduced me to that belief?

_____

Do I still believe it? Why or why not?

_____

Make your list as detailed or broad as you like. Revise it as you continue to learn and grow and **use it to create your personal Life Philosophy**. Lok how far you have already come!

Take the time to really contemplate your future. How would you like it to look? Are there things you have wanted to try but would not allow yourself to attempt previously, due to your religious beliefs? Write a list and start researching how you can turn those dreams into reality!

A NOTE ABOUT COMING OUT AS A NONBELIEVER TO LOVED ONES

As you can see, there is a lot to consider when it comes to exploring and embracing identities.

As we experiment with new identities, it can feel tempting to blurt out our *extimony* to others, especially if feeling pressured by them to tow the religious line. I urge you to proceed with caution and compassion.

It may come as a tremendous shock to your loved ones that you no longer believe – especially if *they* still do. You will be well served to first sit with your trepidation over what coming out as a nonbeliever may cost you.

Considerations must include your personal safety, first and foremost. Would coming out as a nonbeliever put you in danger? If you are not concerned about physical danger, are you beholden to religious family members financially or for a place to live or for childcare?

It is wise to have a safety net in place for yourself before coming out as a nonbeliever: Savings in the bank, a place to stay should you be asked to leave – you might even want to consult a lawyer if you have concerns regarding your marriage and potential custody issues with your children.

Once you have faced those fears, you will be in a more grounded space, and better able to proceed with integrity and compassion, knowing that religious loved ones will fear that they are losing you. You are divulging information that may significantly change your relationship with them.

Understand that you have no control over how others will feel or react to your news. Expect them to react with some emotion – and do your best not to take it personally. You might tell them how much they mean to you and that you deeply desire to maintain the relationship. Encourage them to ask you questions about your deconversion journey if you want to tell them more about it.

Few of us respond positively when first presented with what we consider to be bad news. If you are coming out to your religious parents with the fact that you no longer believe in their religion, remember that a parent's prime directive is to protect their offspring – and if they believe in Hell, they now see you as being in utter peril.

Try to perceive a strong reaction as evidence of their love and concern. If safety is not an issue but you feel the need to set boundaries with religious loved ones, do so as lovingly as possible. Healthy boundaries do not always need to be set in stone; they may have an element of flexibility depending on circumstance. You do not have to write off your partner or parent or friend based on their immediate response to your revelation.

Down the road, your loved ones may decide that they prefer to have you in their life, even though you no longer believe as they do. Be compassionate and honest, doing your best to honor both of you amid a difficult process. Reach out to a professional *secular* counsellor for support if needed.

CRAFTING YOUR LIFE PHILOSOPHY

Fundamentalism disempowers us by teaching that we are hostages to God's will. The truth is, *you have the power to create a life that is meaningful and beautiful to you* – as long as you are willing to do the work. Set a goal, break down your steps into small, bite-sized morsels, and consistently work towards it. Unsure where to start? Meet with someone who has already done what you are interested in and ask them about it.

Learn from others! Case in point: I had no idea what was involved in podcasting until I'd been a guest on other podcasts and became a co-host myself.

Considering more general life philosophies, we might explore ideas like optimism, being present, and simplicity. We take into account what we have learned and experienced already; what has or has not worked for us.

You might have encountered some life-philosophy quotes like:

- *Don't sweat the small stuff*
- *Trust in gods but tie up your camel*
- *Fall down seven times, stand up eight*
- *When someone shows you their true colors, don't paint over them*
- *Be yourself; everyone else is taken.*

Here are two of my favorite Life Philosophies (links for both are available in Module 3 Resources)

Steve Jobs' philosophy, taken from his 2005 commencement speech to the graduating class at Stanford: https://sourcesofinsight.com/steve-jobs-life-advice/

"Your time is limited, so don't waste it living someone else's life. Don't be trapped by dogma – which is living with the results of other people's thinking. Don't let the noise of others' opinions drown out your own inner voice. And most important, have the courage to follow your heart and intuition. They somehow already know what you truly want to become."

Michael Dowd's philosophy from his piece called My TEDx Talk: Reality Reconciles Science and Religion *https://www.huffpost.com/entry/tedx-talk-reality-reconci_b_5513264*

I am an evidential mystic. Reality is my God. Evidence is my scripture. Big history is my creation story, and ecology is my theology. Integrity is my salvation and ensuring a just and healthy future for the planet is my mission. (HuffPost June 20, 2014)

LET THE FUN BEGIN!

First, we explore and investigate. Then, we experiment. Experimenting may include attending a Meet-Up Group related to your interest or joining an online community. While it may be tempting, *I recommend resisting the urge to make grand public declarations about your new identity.* What's the hurry? Take time to test drive the new you. Be open to any critiques that you may have; investigate them and adjust accordingly. Do not fall back into fundamentalist black-and-white thinking. Immaturity shouts "It's all or nothing," but maturity knows better.

Monitor your attachment level to new ideologies. There is a difference between something logically making sense and something emotionally resonating with you—and it is the logic that is more trustworthy. Fundamentalism employs many psychological mind-control techniques that blunt and twist your emotions. When you experience a visceral reaction to something, sit with it and investigate your response.

Keep in mind that if you have children still living at home, they will be impacted by your new identity. *Do your best to remain compassionate and respectful of others while building your new self.*

Lastly, remember that zealots tend to come across as obnoxious. Keep this in mind as you reconstruct your identity and make it public. Do not waste time and energy trying to convince others to be something they are not. Likewise, you don't have to defend your own beliefs. Do your research, find what resonates with you, and respect yourself. If you receive information that merits changing your views, do it. If we are wise, we will continue to evolve.

Module 4C THOUGHTFUL WORDS

Life can only be understood backward, but it must be lived forwards.
—Soren Kierkegaard

The only way to deal with an unfree world is to become so absolutely free that your very existence is an act of rebellion.
—Albert Camus

No man ever steps in the same river twice, for it's not the same river and he's not the same man.
—Heraclitus

Do not spoil what you have by desiring what you have not; remember that what you now have was once among the things you only hoped for.
—Epicurus

How you feel about me is none of my business.
– 12-step aphorism

JANICE SELBIE, RPC

Module 4 Links and Resources

MODULE FIVE

INTEGRATING YOUR LOSSES:
Reframing and Rituals

This part gets you acquainted with the cognitive tool of reframing, helping you further finalize your divorce and move on to your healthy new life.

There was a time during our separation when I needed to cut back on communication with my former husband. It was too painful and hampered my ability to move ahead. We remained living together for over a year into our separation, which was emotionally challenging for us both. I had to move out.

Eventually, we were able to resume harmonious interactions. Since we have two children together, one of whom has fragile health, we needed to resolve our issues as expediently as possible. This required us to behave like mature adults, even when we felt more like cranky toddlers. In the end, I believe this fostered our ability to accept and move on from our divorce.

What does it mean to integrate losses? **When we truly understand our loss and can once again enjoy life, we have integrated our loss**. We do not forget about the loss, and we may even still feel sad about it, but we are no longer preoccupied with painful, crippling thoughts of it. After we have integrated our loss, it is easier for us to participate in life again. We may still be subject to *"grief bursts,"* especially on former holy days that were once deeply significant to us. This is normal, and it will pass.

REFRAMING

While there is no way to speed up grief and the integration process, there are ways to make the burden more manageable. Something that worked for me, and which I employ frequently in my life, is **cognitive reframing**. Using our thoughts, we put the situation into a new frame so that we can see it differently. In our case, we will employ this device on issues related to our Divorce from religion.

We must challenge our automatic negative thoughts. While we can't change the facts of a situation, changing the way we think about those facts allows us to see the situation in a better light, fostering a more hopeful outlook and encouraging resilience.

This involves replacing negative, injurious thoughts with more responsible ones, such as *"What has this experience taught me?"* or *"What can I learn from this?"* Our emotional tone shifts as we change our thinking, potentially impacting the very meaning we ascribe to our circumstance (the Divorce).

Fundamentalism strips us of our ability to choose, telling us that things *must be* a certain way. The truth is, you have the power to reframe your experience from a negative and draining one to a potentially powerful one that you can use to expand your life.

Try using the reframing tool the next time an issue comes up at work (or elsewhere in your life). *Rather than seeing it as a problem or barrier, tell yourself that it is a challenge to be met.* Can you feel the energetic difference? Language matters! If you are unfamiliar with reframing, it can take a concerted effort at first; but the more you use it, the easier it becomes. Some of you likely use reframing naturally, unaware that you are even doing it.

The reframing process calls for us to see our circumstances in a new light, requiring that we recognize potentially positive aspects of the situation. If your Divorce from religion was very recent, your pain may feel too fresh to allow you to see anything potentially positive or helpful in your experience. In that case, you might try and view it as an outsider (devoid of religious and emotional trauma) might see it.

Reframing is an important skill to master because it helps us change loss into challenge and, ultimately, to transfigure challenge into the potential to live life more fully.

A well-known master of reframing was Holocaust survivor and psychiatrist Dr. Viktor Frankl, whose loved ones were murdered in concentration camps during WWII. Most of his fellow imprisoned Jews also died, unable to endure the emotional, mental, and physical torture of life in the death camps. To aid in Dr. Frankl's survival, he mentally rehearsed lessons to teach his students about his terrifying Holocaust experiences. He reframed the horror into teachable lessons. Mentally preparing these lessons kept his mind active and gave him a reason to live. Upon his liberation, Dr. Frankl went on to give those lectures, as well as write several books about his experiences.

Because the ability to reframe is so valuable, I want you to practice it and look for every opportunity to incorporate it into your life.

Here is my brief LIST OF REFRAMING EXAMPLES:

"I am a failure at marriage and Christianity"

became

"I had two precious children with someone I respected and loved. I was a solid Christian while I believed."

"I feel like a fool for being a gullible fundamentalist."

became

"When I realized the truth, I left. Now I understand the dangers of fundamentalism."

* * * * *

"I can't trust my own decisions because I was deceived for so long."

became

"As soon as my knowledge increased, I made the right choice. I can educate myself and trust my own decisions."

* * * * *

"It is too hard to make new friends. I will always be alone"

became

"I love the freedom I have to make friends with anyone I choose!"

WHAT DID YOU LEARN?

Part of reframing involves looking back at your time in religion and trying to redeem (pun wickedly intended!) any value from it. **What threads of meaning or purpose can you retrieve and take with you?** Did you learn anything non-religious that is worth taking into your new life?

Here are a few things I learned during, or as a result of, my decades as a fundamentalist Christian that remain with me today:

- I love singing and am good at it

- I am a natural encourager of others
- I enjoy writing
- I am compassionate
- I must take responsibility for investigating and not just believe because others do or because they say that something is the truth
- My freedom is more valuable to me than anything else, and I will preserve it at all costs
- The same words may hold different meanings, depending on who is using them. For example: *Grace*, *saved*, and *love* hold different meanings for me as a nonbeliever than they did when I was religious.

Take the time to challenge your automatic negative thoughts (ANTs) and reframe them. **Write down some of your powerful ANTs, along with your re-frame, and review them.** This will help change your neural pathways and habits more quickly.

You will have learned lessons about yourself, your community, your beliefs, and more during your time spent in fundamentalism. Writing this **reframing list** can help ease your pain and get you used to reframing.

Refer to my LIST OF REFRAMING EXAMPLES above to create your own here:

_____

_____

_____

_____

INTEGRATING YOUR LOSSES: REFRAMING AND RITUALS

RITUALS

We touched on this in Module 2, under *Tips to Help with Grief*. Rituals acknowledge that we are leaving one part of our life and moving into another; they both punctuate and clarify for us. They can help commemorate the past and celebrate the future.

One aspect of religious life we may miss is liturgy, especially at certain times of the year. I cried every Easter morning for years following my Divorce from religion, because it had been such an important time for me previously. The tradition amongst my denomination was to greet others with the phrase "He is risen!" to which we would reply "He is risen, indeed." How I loved uttering those words and feeling a connection with Christian believers through the ages. The loss of that one small ritual was profound for me.

Likewise, a handmade Nativity calendar I did with my daughters throughout their childhood was a significant and much-anticipated ritual for us and one that we missed when I stopped believing. Even something as simple as enjoying Christmas carols was a loss for me post-belief. For years, I had to turn off the radio when religious carols came on, or I was reduced to tears. The pain of my loss was real and deep.

These days, I enjoy celebrating the winter and spring solstices. Doing so helps me feel connected to the great sea of humanity that has been part of the Earth for millennia. No longer religious, my new husband has developed a daily ritual that involves scattering coffee grounds in each direction and honoring both what was and what will be, as well as those who will come and have gone from his life.

Develop rituals that make sense to you. Some examples include:

- Writing a poem
- Preparing and eating a special meal

- Talking with a specific friend or visiting a specific location on a certain day
- Creating, burning, or burying something representative of your religious days.

The possibilities for personal rituals are as unique and creative as each individual. When I Divorced Religion, I found writing and speaking publicly about it to be very liberating. My ceremony involved swapping out all of my religious iconography and Christian books for ones that were a more accurate representation of where I was at that time: Crystals, Buddhas, and inspirational quotes. These days I'm surrounded by photos and paintings of nature and books about science, humanism, feminism, and indigenous cultures from around the world.

LIST OF RITUALS & PRACTICES

Start a list of rituals and practices you used to enjoy when religious, along with potential new traditions to try:

_____

_____

_____

_____

_____

_____

_____

_____

This section on reframing and ritual would be incomplete without encouraging readers to explore Joseph Campbell's book The Power of Myth (Anchor 1991). You can also watch The Power of Myth series on YouTube (*See Module 5 Resources for link*). This series was extremely helpful to me during both my religious deconstruction and my reconstruction. I felt flooded with awe and relief as Professor Campbell passionately and clearly explained various myths from around the world, including Christian ones, as simply being metaphors relating to the human condition.

Module 5 THOUGHTFUL WORDS

We must die to one life before we can live another.
—Anatole France

I look upon the gift of my life as a wondrous journey.
—Maureen Brady

Study hard what interests you the most in the most undisciplined, irreverent, and original manner possible.
—Richard Feynmann

Self-education is, I firmly believe, the only kind of education there is.
—Isaac Asimov

RESOURCES

(Links available in Module 5 Resources on my website)

Reframing:

- How Cognitive Reframing Works, by LCSW Amy Morin
- Reframing: The Transformative Power of Suffering, by Linda and Charlie Bloom (Psychology Today, December 14, 2017)

Rituals:

To learn more about incorporating rituals into your post-religious life, I recommend:

- *For Small Creatures Such as We: Rituals for Finding Meaning in Our Unlikely World*, by Sasha Sagan (G.P. Putnam's Sons, 2021)
- *13 Fascinating Winter Solstice Traditions Around the World*, by Tina Dovito (Reader's Digest Feb 29, 2024)
- *Nine Ways People Celebrate the Summer Solstice Around the World*, by Kristin Pope (Smithsonian Magazine June 20, 2023)

Module 5 Links and Resources

MODULE SIX

PLENTY OF FISH: Finding and Building Your New Communities

This module looks at developing intentional communities to make your new life functional and enjoyable.

Divorce hurts us in every way: Physiologically, mentally, emotionally. As one astute observer put it:

> *Divorce is the psychological equivalent of a triple coronary bypass.*
> —Mary Kay Blakely

Formerly simple tasks become fraught with pain as we process the fullness of our losses. I didn't just lose my husband and best friend, I also lost my home, my business office, my identity, and my dream of our future together.

One of the hardest losses, though, was friendships with other married couples. It is like a chill goes through the crowd, and they become fearful that divorce will be contagious. When it comes to leaving our religious community, Believers seem to fear that our apostasy may infect them, so they stop interacting with us.

PLENTY OF FISH: FINDING AND BUILDING NEW COMMUNITIES

I had to learn to navigate the world as a single person in my 40s, after 20 years of being committed to just one other person. It was a huge learning curve, to say the least.

Dating can feel daunting, but it is also an opportunity to remake yourself, presenting an updated image of who you are and what you want in a partner.

Being shut out of their former community is the most common lament that I hear when speaking with those who have Divorced Religion. We have lost the one-stop shop that met our needs on multiple levels, from childcare to purpose to social interaction.

There is a reason that I have subtitled this module "Finding and building your new *communities*," plural. Now, instead of having all your needs met in one handy place, **research, courage, and effort are required to meet these needs in different places**. Like a patchwork quilt, you will gather your new friends around each different need or interest that you have.

Start by listing some of the needs you have since Divorcing Religion, such as socializing, purpose, education, creative endeavors, etc.:

_____

_____

_____

Some of your needs can likely be met by utilizing online resources, such as **Facebook, Threads, Reddit, Bluesky, Instagram,** and **TikTok**. Facebook (FB) helped me build my business and reconnect with old friends, as well as make new ones by joining various FB groups. I also use FB as a way to invite locals to attend events that I host or to suggest groups that I might enjoy.

YouTube (YT) is a powerful and important option for those of us recovering from religion because there are so many great channels offering useful information. Whatever you are curious about or wherever you have knowledge gaps, a YT channel can help! If you are looking for a safe starting place to learn about religious trauma syndrome and recovery resources, come visit my channel: YouTube.com/@cometocort

Whatever your religious background, you can find others on social media who have also left and are looking to support one another.

One caveat here: Beware hateful places on the internet. *When we are angry, it is easy to resonate with other angry people.* Like attracts like. There is a big difference, however, between unproductive outrage and productive anger that leads to change. Groups filled with the former lead to burnout; groups filled with the latter feel encouraging.

Some of your needs may be better met face-to-face. Here are some **ways to start building your real-life communities:**

- Miss singing? Join a local non-religious choir or start attending/hosting karaoke nights and house concerts.

- Miss playing your instrument on Sunday mornings? Join your local symphony or place an ad seeking other musicians in your community classified ads.

- Miss discussing important topics? Join a book club or a humanist, atheist, or skeptic's group.

- Miss "missions" trips? Join a secular organization that does humanitarian work around the globe.

- Miss being energized by youth or feeling good by serving elders? Volunteer. Currently, I volunteer as president of my local atheists, skeptics, and humanists' association. In the past, I have volunteered at my local Hospice, library, hospital, Alzheimer's Society, Suicide/Crisis hotline, homeless shelter, skating rink, and more. Even airports need volunteers to help confused flyers find their way to the right terminal or simply find a meal. Volunteering is a great way to start interacting with folks outside of your former religious group – and you never know the connections you might make.

- Celebrate birthdays, graduations, weddings, divorces, career changes, loan repayments, finishing chemotherapy, and anything else! No victory is too small to celebrate.

- Miss group events providing a sense of community? Here are some to try.

    - *Sunday Assembly*: "Sunday Assembly is the world's fastest-growing secular community. We join together to celebrate life..." Sunday Assembly is a great way to meet with others, in person, who have left religion behind and want to enjoy life to the full.

    - The *Oasis Network* touts itself as "a place for the nonreligious to come together to celebrate the Human experience."

    - *Unitarian Universalists* are a nontheistic group that you may also enjoy, "grounded in the humanistic teachings of the world's religions." *Check out Module 6 Resources for links to Sunday Assembly, Oasis, and Unitarian Universalist Association.*

- Try your hand at new activities: Hiking, darts, billiards, crafting, bowling... You have nothing to lose by trying new things. Give yourself permission to relax, be imperfect, laugh at yourself, and make friends with similar interests.

MEETUP GROUPS

Have you heard about Meetups? They are terrific – and can be found around the world! According to Wikipedia, **Meetup** is a service used to organize online groups that host in-person events for people with similar interests. As of 2017, there were about 225,000 Meetup groups in 180 countries with about 35 million Meetup users!

No matter how obscure your interest, there's a good chance you can find a Meetup group to help you connect in real life with others who share it. I have used Meetup groups in my town to connect with other writers, hikers, skeptics, humanists, would-be artists, and people interested in attending theatrical presentations who just did not want to go alone. If you can't find a group for your interest, start one of your own. *See Module 6 Resources for Meetup information*

FACEBOOK GROUPS

Facebook Groups for religious recovery abound. Just type the name of your former religious group into the search bar and see what pops up. Lurk long enough to get a sense of how healthy the group is. Some "religious trauma recovery" groups have a combined membership of those who have fully rejected religion and those who remain religious, which can be problematic. Remember: You are allowed to leave any group you have joined, and you don't even need to give a reason.

PODCASTS

I LOVE podcasts! Essentially, they are individual radio shows that you can access any time of day, on pretty much every topic imaginable. Podcasts are a delightful and helpful result of technology. I listen to them while driving, walking, cooking, and cleaning. I like them so much, I started my own: The Divorcing Religion Podcast.

Some of my favorites are podcasts about deconverting from fundamentalist religions and other high-demand groups and cults, but I also enjoy podcasts about advertising, true crime, comedy, and more. I use a podcast app on my phone, but you can also just listen over the internet on a computer.

An internet browser will be your closest ally in finding and building your communities after Divorcing Religion. Around the world or in your neighborhood, others are waiting to meet someone just like you, to expand their world and take the sting of loneliness away. Whether for hobbies or help, the world is at your fingertips.

Religion robs us of our autonomy and independence, making us dependent on the church. We were prevented from meaningful interactions with those outside of our belief system and discouraged from meeting our own needs.

BE BRAVE

Now is the time to joyfully take ownership of your life and meet your own needs. You are both 100% free and 100% responsible for your life, and it can be as full or spacious as you choose. *Educating yourself and spending energy on building your new life are the best ways to recover after Divorce.* It is not a burden, but an empowering, liberating challenge!

Remember, nothing is carved in stone; you may join a group and then decide it's not for you. If that's the case, you can simply stop attending. You are under no obligation to continue attending or to explain your absence. The important thing is to get out there and try.

You never know who you may meet in the attempt, or what helpful resource they may direct you to. Religion's commodities are fear and shame – but they do not rule you any longer. **Do what you must to meet your own needs and build a meaningful life of purpose for**

yourself. Set a goal, break down your steps into bite-sized morsels, and consistently work towards it.

Unsure where to start? Learn from others! Meet with someone who has already done what you are interested in and ask them about it. Case in point: I wanted to reach as many people as possible to educate them about religious trauma syndrome and the recovery help available. Not content with just 1:1 work or group work or my conferences, I determined a podcast and YouTube channel could help spread my message – which is part of what makes life meaningful to me.

I had no idea what was involved in podcasting until I'd been a guest on other shows and became a co-host myself of The Godless Moms, with my friend Courtney. I asked questions and built up my confidence until I was ready to launch the Divorcing Religion Podcast, which has been downloaded about 82,000 times since launching in the autumn of 2022 (two years ago).

Since launching the Conference on Religious Trauma YouTube channel (where I post prior CORT and Shameless Sexuality Conference sessions, as well as Divorcing Religion Podcast episodes) in March of 2022, my channel has had over 323,000 views and now boasts over 4,200 subscribers. Knowing little about YouTube, I reached out to experts for their professional knowledge, and it is paying off.

Sometimes things won't work out, and this is true for all humans. When this occurs, dust yourself off, spend some time investigating what happened – and move on to your next adventure.

15 Books

Here are some books that may help you understand your own experiences with religion and the intersection between politics, culture, and Christianity:

1. *Bounded Choice*, by Dr. Janja Lalich (University of California Press 2004)

2. *Fantasyland: How America Went Haywire - A 500 Year History*, by Kurt Andersen (Random House 2017)

3. *Goodbye Jesus: An Evangelical Preacher's Journey Beyond Faith*, by Tim Sledge (Insighting Growth Publications Inc. 2018)

4. *Holy Terror: The Fundamentalist War on America's Freedoms in Religion, Politics, and Our Private Lives*, by Flo Conway and Jim Siegelman (Doubleday 1982)

5. *Jesus, Interrupted, Revealing the Hidden Contradictions in the Bible* by Bart Ehrman (Harper One 2010)

6. *Leaving the Fold: A guide for former fundamentalists and others leaving their religion* by Dr. Marlene Winell (Apocryphile 2007)

7. *Sex & God: How Religion Distorts Sexuality*, by Dr. Darrel Ray (IPC Press 2012)

8. *Take Back Your Life: Recovering from Cults and Abusive Relationships*, by Janja Lalich and Madeleine Tobias (Bay Tree Publishing; 2 edition Aug. 17, 2006)

9. *Taking America Back for God: Christian Nationalism in the United States*, by Andrew L. Whitehead and Samuel L. Perry (Oxford University Press 2020)

10. *The Flag and the Cross: White Christian Nationalism and the Threat to American Democracy*, by Philip Gorski and Samuel L. Perry (Oxford University Press 2022)

11. *The God Virus: How Religion Affects Our Lives and Culture*, by Dr. Darrel Ray (IPC Press 2009)

12. *The Power Worshippers: Inside the Dangerous Rise of Religious Nationalism*, by Katherine Stewart (Bloomsbury Publishing 2022)

13. *Trusting Doubt: A Former Evangelical Looks at Old Beliefs In a New Light*, by Dr. Valerie Tarico (Oracle Institute Press; 2nd ed. edition Sept. 1, 2017)

14. *Walking Free from the Trauma of Coercive, Cultic, and Spiritual Abuse*, by Dr. Gillie Jenkinson (Routledge 2023)

15. *Wayward*, by Alice Greczyn (River Grove Books 2021)

15 Podcasts

1. Cults Podcast, with Greg Polcyn & Vanessa Richardson
2. Conspirituality, with Derek Beres, Matthew Remski, Julian Walker
3. Dismantling Doctrine, with Dr. Clint Heacock
4. Divorcing Religion, with Janice Selbie
5. Feet of Clay: Confessions of the Cult Sisters, with Tracey and Sharon
6. Free Thought Radio & Podcast (Freedom from Religion Foundation)
7. Gaslit Nation, with Andrea Chalupa
8. How to Heretic, with Mark, Dan, and Doug
9. IndoctriNATION, with Dr. Rachel Bernstein
10. I was a Teenage Fundamentalist, with Brian McDowell and Troy Waller

11. Recovering from Religion Podcast (RfRx), with Kara Griffin
12. The Influence Continuum, with Dr. Steven Hassan
13. The Thinking Atheist, with Seth Andrews
14. Voices of Deconversion Podcast, with Steve Hilliker
15. Yasmine Mohammed, with Yasmine Mohammed

15 YouTube Channels

These channels provide valuable content for atheists, skeptics, and anyone interested in exploring topics related to atheism, religion, science, and critical thinking on YouTube.

1. Cosmic Skeptic, with Alex O'Connor
2. Divorcing Religion, with Janice Selbie
3. Genetically Modified Skeptic, with Drew McCoy
4. Godless Engineer, with John Gleason
5. Holy Koolaid, with Thomas Westbrook
6. Journey Free, with Dr. Marlene Winell
7. Kurzgesagt
8. Paulogia, with Paul Ens
9. Sensibly Speaking & Critical Conversations, with Chris Shelton
10. Smarter Every Day
11. The Line
12. The Thinking Atheist, with Seth Andrews
13. Thinking is Power, with Melanie Trecek-King

14. Valerie Tarico - God's Emotions series
15. Vox

15 Interesting Websites

**Links available under Module 6 Resources*

1. Amnesty International
2. Black Nonbelievers
3. Cult Education
4. Dare to Doubt
5. Divorcing Religion
6. Freedom from Religion Foundation
7. Free Hearts Free Minds
8. Godless Mom
9. Human Rights Watch
10. Humanists International
11. Journey Free
12. Recovering from Religion
13. Rights and Religions Forum
14. Secular Coalition for America
15. Upworthy

This list is by no means exhaustive! There are countless groups (online and in person), podcasts, websites, and books that may be incredibly helpful to you. Ready... Set... GROW!

Module 6 THOUGHTFUL WORDS

Not in their goals but in their transitions are people great.
—RW Emerson

We are called to be architects of the future, not its victims.
—Buckminster Fuller

Tell me, what is it you plan to do with your one wild and precious life?
—Mary Oliver

My strength lies solely in my tenacity.
—Louis Pasteur

Module 6 Links and Resources

The final module of the Divorcing Religion Survival Handbook is very important. We have previously fallen prey to an insidious and toxic worldview, and we must take care to ensure that it does not happen again.

MODULE SEVEN

MIND CONTROL: Don't Let an Old Flame Burn You Twice

Mind control typically refers to the manipulation or influence of an individual's thoughts, beliefs, emotions, or behaviors. This manipulation can range from subtle forms of persuasion to more coercive or manipulative tactics aimed at exerting control over a person's mind and actions. Mind control techniques can include psychological manipulation, propaganda, and other forms of influence that shape an individual's thoughts and behaviors to the point of creating a new identity desired by the controller.

I will never know the person I might have been had my mind not been hijacked (indoctrinated) by my parents' religious beliefs. My personality and behaviors developed around those beliefs which were spoon-fed to me from Day 1. Those who fall into cults (religious and non-religious) and conspiracy groups, whether in adolescence or adulthood, suffer a similar fate of being deceived, indoctrinated, and taken over by their new ideology. Fundamentalists and fanatics are chillingly similar to zombies: Unable to think for themselves and bent on replicating.

Check out Module 7 Resources for a link to David McDermott's helpful website examining mind control.

Before Divorcing Religion, we were discouraged from thinking critically and encouraged to think only through the lens of our specific religion. For me, this meant rejecting scientific ideas like evolution without due consideration. If my pastor said it and other Christians believed it (especially famous ones like James Dobson), I believed it, too. As it turns out, neither my parents nor my religious teachers taught me *how* to think; instead, they simply taught me *what* to think.

We are creatures of attachment; first to caregivers, then to ideologies and beliefs. If we are indoctrinated with ideologies as children, receiving them from our caregivers, we have *no choice* but to believe them because our survival depends on it.

When I was finally able to break free from religion's suffocating grip, I became keenly interested in fundamentalism, fanaticism, and psychological techniques employed by religious groups to increase persuasion (AKA mind control). These tactics are varied, complex, and effective; I do not claim to be an expert. I encourage you to perform your own research and educate yourself.

Critical thinking involves analyzing and evaluating information, arguments, and evidence logically and systematically. It requires the ability to question assumptions, consider different perspectives, and recognize biases.

Critical thinkers are adept at identifying flaws in reasoning, assessing the credibility of sources, and making reasoned judgments based on evidence and sound reasoning. They are open-minded people, intellectually curious, and willing to revise their beliefs in light of new information.

The ability to think critically is essential for making informed decisions, solving complex problems, and engaging in meaningful discourse. In short, it is exactly what religious devotees are trained to avoid. Instead, they are fed logical fallacies.

A **logical fallacy** is **a mistake in reasoning that invalidates an argument**. As hardcore religious Believers, we fell prey to some doozies - and we weren't even aware of it because we were so thoroughly indoctrinated. The most obvious one is *an argument from authority* which involves insisting that a claim is true simply because a supposed expert says that it is so.

For example: "Reverend Strong says that a woman who never had sex got pregnant. He is a learned man, so it must be true!" Another common one is *circular reasoning*. An example: "Why believe the Bible? Because it is the Word of God. Why believe in God? Because the Bible says He exists."

A simple exercise taken from Dr. Marlene Caroselli illustrates the limitations we encounter when beliefs prevent critical thinking:

The following combination of letters represents a sentence from which one particular vowel has been removed. If you can figure out what that vowel is and re-insert it eleven times, in eleven different places, you will be able to determine what the sentence is saying.

VRYFINXMP

LARXCDSW

HATWXPCT

Most problem-solvers soon realize the missing letter is "e," probably because the word "very" seems to jump out at them. They work hard to construct the sentence with "very" as its first word. "Very" is not the first word, however; "every" is. **When conviction and determination prevent us from exploring alternative options, we limit our potential for thinking critically.**

The whole sentence actually reads:

"Every fine exemplar exceeds what we expect."

(Reproduced from 50 Activities for Developing Critical Thinking Skills copyright 2009, Marlene Caroselli. Used by permission of the publisher: HRD Press, Inc. www.hrdpress.com)

Additional resources on critical thinking can be found at the end of this module.

Fundamentalism is the gateway to Fanaticism

For this section, I greatly appreciated Kalmer Marimaa's 2011 piece The Many Faces of Fanaticism (2011, Tartu Theological Seminary). The link to his article is under Module 7 Resources.

For this module, the terms *fundamentalism* and *fanaticism* will be used interchangeably.

While not identical, fundamentalism and fanaticism are closely related to each other. The main difference is that fanaticism is behaviorally based; it is one's *behavior* that merits the title of fanatic. Fundamentalism is not initially action-based but is rather an *attitude* and *manner of thinking*.

Fundamentalists generally idealize the past and desire its restoration in some way, a dream that feels secure to members (making it especially attractive to parents and seniors). Fanaticism, on the other hand, does not necessarily idealize the past and often appeals to youth who are seeking drama and action. Both groups avoid critical thinking, eventually replacing their passion for an ideology with obsession. In other words, *the object of their devotion is eventually superseded by the act of devotion itself.*

This is where **identity enmeshment** comes into play. Critical thinking tends to weaken the fantasy that fundamentalists and fanatics have built their beliefs upon and their lives around. While their origins may be different, it does not take much for fundamentalists to become fanatical in their behavior. **Fanatical attachment to an ideology leads to the original concepts of the ideology becoming less important than the need to impose it on others** (I.e., to subjugate). Fanatical devotion to even *good* concepts is harmful. Extreme devotion to any ideology creates division. The deeper our level of attachment, the harsher the division – until, eventually, we stop seeing the humanity of those on the other side.

I was not "just" a Christian: I was a born again, baptized in the Holy Spirit, ready-to-be-a-martyr Christian fundamentalist, rebuking the devil wherever I found him. I had both of my newborn daughters "dedicated" to Jesus and His service, whatever the cost. I read to them from Foxe's Book of Martyrs (by John Foxe, 1563) so that they would be aware of the highest price that evil, dangerous non-Christians might demand of them someday – and that their faith and allegiance must never waiver. I saw value only in a Christian identity.

The grip our beliefs hold over us is important. Being unaware of the depth of our attachments to a given belief can bring misery to us and those around us (I was a textbook example of this). Being aware of our attachments, however, gives us power. Awareness provides the freedom to decide whether or not we will continue holding our beliefs. Our power lies in our ability to choose. When we fail to see that we have a choice, it is no longer us holding our belief; it is at that point that *our belief is holding us*. We are no longer free.

Spiritual journeys often start with curious seekers exploring and appreciating different flavors of spirituality. Once a seeker becomes fanatical, however, the religion itself becomes more important than the god it promotes.

As a fundamentalist, I could not even entertain the thought of rejecting evangelical Christianity. My thorough and unwavering attachment to it robbed me of my ability to think clearly and critically; I just could not imagine myself without the label of "Christian" attached.

My belief constructed my entire narrative about reality. When I was devoutly religious, much of my energy was invested in proving and defending that my interpretation of God and scripture were correct. I became so entrenched in my belief that no room remained for growth or change.

Going forward, having Divorced Religion, I will do my best to listen to others; but I will receive their information with cautious skepticism - knowing that they, too, are attached to their own beliefs.

For growth to occur, we need to separate the belief from our devotion to it, so we can examine it truthfully. Consistently questioning our own beliefs - what they are, where they came from, and why we believe them – is what will keep us from becoming a hostage to them. Holding beliefs loosely allows us freedom of choice.

As William James wisely stated: "We have to live today by what truth we can get today and be ready tomorrow to call it falsehood." Strong adherence to a belief obscures our vision; and when our perspective is limited, so are our options. The ties that bind can become the ties that strangle.

QUESTIONS TO ASK ABOUT YOUR BELIEFS:

1. What do I believe about X?
2. Who imparted that belief to me?
3. How is my belief in X controlling me?
4. Is X true and verifiable?
5. Do I still need my belief in X?

WHO JOINS A CULT (religious or otherwise)

- Those born into it or indoctrinated at a young age, before developing critical thinking skills
- Vulnerable people who have been alienated, disenfranchised, or victims of trauma (many of whom fall into addiction and seek help through church-run addiction recovery groups)
- Those experiencing an identity crisis (e.g. youth, young adults, those going through a divorce or newly widowed, etc.)
- Good people who want to make a difference

WHY PEOPLE JOIN

- Seeking security
- Seeking identity
- Feeling frustrated with their lot in life
- Lack of purpose
- Loneliness
- Desperation/Neediness
- Hope (false promises) that either they can be changed, or they can change the world through the cult

WHAT KEEPS CONVERTS TRAPPED

- Comfort, security, fantasy
- **Fear of:** Abandonment, annihilation, apocalypse, embarrassment, failure, Hell
- **Feeling special/elect/superior**: They ALONE have the truth

- **Guilt/Shame:** Sacrifices were made for you/You made a vow/ You converted others
- **Isolation/insulation:** Prohibited from questioning group dogma/Prohibited from relationships outside of the group
- **Limited education, skills, or resources** (especially financial support)
- **Social conformity:** Charismatic leadership, group pressure, community

COMMON PSYCHOLOGICAL MANIPULATION TACTICS

Fundamentalist religious groups and other cults (including human potential cults, political cults, terrorist organizations, and more) employ a wide array of psychological manipulation tactics to persuade people to join. These tactics can over-ride a person's free will and critical thinking. Unwitting and well-intentioned victims fall prey to such tactics, which can include deception, coercion, hypnosis, flattery, and more.

Psychological manipulation tactics I have experienced in evangelical churches:

- ✞ Altar calls
- ✞ Charismatic leaders
- ✞ Confession encouraged (personal disclosure can lead to feeling socially bonded/beholden to a group or individual and pressured to remain)
- ✞ Group singing and prayers (which induce bonding)

- ✞ Mood lighting (lowered lighting during altar calls and prayer times)
- ✞ Mood music (special words, volume, and even certain chord progressions)
- ✞ Speaking in tongues, ecstatic dancing, holy laughter
- ✞ Tissue boxes strategically placed in pews (providing expectation of emotional release)

Together, these can activate a state of ecstasy (the philosophical notion of "standing outside one's self"), which encourages groupthink and losing your sense of self.

With regard to corporate singing, there has been some good research about brain synchronization and music. This most commonly occurs in religious and military settings, where group members must bond with each other, trust their leaders, and share a common goal. In their article *Synchrony in the periphery: Inter-subject correlation of physiological responses during live music concerts*, the authors note:

"Overall, our results show that specific music features induce similar physiological responses across audience members in a concert context, which are linked to arousal, engagement, and familiarity."[10]

Interestingly, "speaking in tongues" and/or chanting can produce heightened emotional arousal – as can spinning, which is practiced by Islamic Whirling Dervishes – and can produce an altered state of consciousness, *making people more prone to suggestion*. Pentecostals, Mormons, and others claim that some of these practices and feelings

---

[10] https://www.nature.com/articles/s41598-021-00492-3?fromPaywallRec=false
Czepiel, A., Fink, L. K., Fink, L. T., Tröndle, M., & Merrill, J. (2021). Synchrony in the periphery: Inter-subject correlation of physiological responses during live music concerts. Scientific Reports, 11(1), 1-16. https://doi.org/10.1038/s41598-021-00492-3

are evidence of the infilling of the Holy Spirit or other supposed proof that believers are on the one right/true/holy path.

For several years, my first husband and I attended a Vineyard Church in Kelowna, B.C., Canada. Over the years we attended, the senior pastor's wife claimed to have developed the gift of prophecy. What made her prophecies memorable was the fact that she shook violently while delivering them. Her name is Stacey Campbell, and she was featured prominently in what became known as "The Toronto Blessing." *Check out the Module 7 Resources for video links of "the prophetess" in action.*

Psychological illusionist Derren Brown has an excellent special called Miracles for Sale, where he uses evangelistic-type techniques on a secular audience to expose the tricks of "faith healers." *See the link in Module 7 Resources.*

QUESTIONS TO ASK

Before joining any group, the *Freedom of Mind* ® *Resource Center* recommends asking questions about the leadership of the group; transparency and information control; group claims and doctrine; and how the group treats children.

For an expanded version of these questions from Freedom of Mind ®, as well as a thorough look at Dr. Steven Hassan's BITE Model © (and a terrific free printable handout) please use the links found under Module 7 Resources.

The BITE Model©

Cult expert Dr. Steven Hassan developed the BITE Model to describe *specific recruitment and control methods used by cults*. "BITE" stands for **B**ehavior, **I**nformation, **T**hought, and **E**motional control. In a nutshell:

BEHAVIOR CONTROL

- Promotes dependence and obedience
- Dictates living arrangements and controls sexuality
- Exploits resources (especially money and time)

INFORMATION CONTROL

- Withholds and distorts information
- Promotes Us-versus-Them mentality
- Discourages or forbids communication with ex-members

THOUGHT CONTROL

- Instills black-versus-white, good-versus-evil thinking
- Prevents critical thinking by use of thought-stopping techniques (distraction, dissuasion, isolation, occupation, carrot and stick)
- Induces hypnosis, trances, and altered levels of consciousness

EMOTIONAL CONTROL

- Instills irrational fears against leaving or even questioning the group
- Promotes guilt and shame
- Teaches that there is no peace or happiness outside of the group

See Module 7 Resources for these two great links:

One of the best websites I have found for learning about cults and cultic thinking is Rick Alan Ross's Cult Education Institute.

From The Visual Capitalist, the November 26, 2021, article *24 Cognitive Biases That are Warping Your Perception of Reality*, by Jeff Desjardins, is also worth reading.

RELIGION AS ADDICTION

Some view religiosity as an addiction. A *process addiction* involves an activity or a behavior that becomes compulsive, rather than a chemical substance. Deep devotion to religion shares some qualities with addiction.

In Dr. Valerie Tarico's insightful article *THE GOD DRUG: WHEN RELIGION BECOMES AN ADDICTION*,[11] she explores when religion crosses over into a harmful obsession.

The following Signs and Symptoms are modified versions of questions asked by mental health professionals to ascertain whether an individual has developed an addiction to a process or substance. They are inspired by Dr. Tarico's article, named above. **Visit Module 7 Resources for the link.**

Religious Addiction - Signs

- Do you use religion to avoid responsibilities?
- Does preoccupation with religion cause you to neglect your job?
- Is your relationship with religion more important to you than your children and family?

---

[11] Pacific Standard Staff; Updated: June 14, 2017, Original: September 2, 2016

- Are you obsessed with rules?
- Does religion keep you isolated from nonreligious friends and activities?
- Do you use religion as an excuse to cut people out of your life or otherwise abuse them?
- Has anyone told you that your devotion to religion is extreme or obsessive?
- Do you give more time or money to religion than you can afford?
- Do you get defensive when someone questions your religion?

Religious Addiction – Symptoms

- Are you preoccupied with sin and the afterlife?
- Do you think sex is shameful or dirty?
- Do you struggle with guilt and use it as a weapon?
- Do you see the world as black and white, without shades of grey?
- Do you and your group tell others how to interpret the Bible?
- Does your religion threaten violence against people who don't follow it?
- Do you use religion to control the behavior of others?
- Do you argue against scientific evidence when it comes to your religion?
- Do you believe you will prosper only "if God wills it," and that if your plan fails, "It wasn't God's will" for it to succeed?

- Do you still display cult/fundamentalist thinking in any area of your life (religious, political, nutritional, environmental, etc.)?
- Do you categorize between "Us" and "Them"?
- Do you characterize nonbelievers like they are all the same, only by negative traits?
- Do you avoid and/or flat-out reject information about the words and actions of those you disagree with?
- Do you fail to consider points of view that differ from your beliefs?
- Do you disapprove of or disassociate from those who depart from your group's position?
- Do you see dissenters and nonbelievers as a problem?
- Do you believe that only your group knows the real truth, and behave self-righteously because of it? Ask someone outside of your group for their thoughts.

CAUTION:

Experiences can brand us emotionally, leaving neurological footprints. This may explain why you seem drawn to "a certain type" of person romantically, even to your detriment. This is a solid reason not to simply use familiar feelings as a barometer to determine whether a situation or philosophy is good or bad.

Your past experience has primed you to repeat it unless you pay careful attention. Bearing that in mind, let us end our time together with a list of what to watch out for as we bravely step into our future, free from the tyranny of fundamentalist religion.

BE WARY OF:

- Groups with a charismatic leader who appears to be narcissistic
- Groups that are authoritarian with a distinct hierarchy/pyramid shape
- Groups that demand a high amount of your resources (time, money, energy)
- Groups that answer questions with circular reasoning through doctrine or dogma, such as: "God says it, I believe it, that settles it"
- Groups that promise you are going to be part of changing the world
- Groups that insist they alone have the answer
- Groups that are authoritarian and try to enforce obedience and control through guilt, shame, fear, social pressure, sleep deprivation, blackmail, or punishment
- Groups that espouse a doctrine of separation
- Groups that try to separate members from the rest of society
- Groups that try to restrict you from receiving outside information
- Groups that discourage critical thinking
- Group members with mentally or emotionally stunted growth, who are easily threatened by questions or other beliefs
- Groups that try to break down your individuality by forced confession

- Groups that try to psychologically manipulate members with mood lighting, music, and shared experiences.

RESOURCES (see Module 7 Resources for links)

BOOKS

Bounded Choice: True Believers and Charismatic Cults, by Dr. Janja Lalich (University of California, 2004)

Combatting Cult Mind Control, by Dr. Steven Hassan (Freedom of Mind Press 2015)

Cults Inside Out, by Rick Alan Ross (CreateSpace Independent Publishing Platform 2014)

Freedom of Mind, by Dr. Steven Hassan (Freedom of Mind Press; 3rd ed. Edition, Feb. 5, 2022)

Take Back Your Life: Recovering from Cults and Abusive Relationships, by Dr. Janja Lalich and Madeleine Tobias (Bay Tree Publishing, 2006)

Thought Reform and the Psychology of Totalism, by Dr. Robert J. Lifton (Norton, New York, 1961; UNC Press reprint 1989)

WEBSITES and ARTICLES about Critical Thinking and Logical Fallacies:

The Thinking Shop - I love their critical thinking cards and posters about fallacies and biases.

Thinking is Power - I interviewed this website's owner on the Divorcing Religion Podcast, and she did not disappoint!

LIFEHACKER: How to Train Your Mind to Think Critically and Form Your Own Opinions, by Thorin Klosowski

The Foundation for Critical Thinking: Critical Thinking in Everyday Life Modified from the book by Paul, R. & Elder, L. (2001).

Psychology Today: How to Learn Critical Thinking, by William R. Klemm, PhD

On Persuading and Resisting Persuasion:

The Website *Influence at Work: Proven Science for Business Success*

- The Principles of Persuasion Aren't Just for Business, by Dr. Robert Cialdini, May 23, 2016
- PsyBlog: 9 Ways Persuasion Can be Resisted, by Dr. Jeremy Dean, July 24, 2022
- Decision-Making Confidence: What is Mind Control? © 2006-2024 by Dr. David Mc Dermott
- PsyBlog: How to Encourage People to Change Their Own Minds, by Dr. Jeremy Dean, May 9, 2012

Module 7 THOUGHTFUL WORDS

Those who cannot change their minds cannot change anything.
—George Bernard Shaw

Conformity is the jailer of freedom and the enemy of growth.
—J.F. Kennedy

One believes things because one has been conditioned to believe them.
—Aldous Huxley

Until you realize how easily it is for your mind to be manipulated, you remain the puppet of someone else's game.
—Evita Ochel

All religions start off as cults. Any religions that justify slavery, killing, oppression, division… are still cults.
—George Banister

Module 7 Links and Resources

FINAL THOUGHTS

Since humans first wondered about the changing seasons in nature and life, we have sought to interpret and explain those changes by constructing stories to ascribe meaning to random events. While such myths describe the human condition metaphorically, many people have unfortunately misinterpreted those myths as facts. Accordingly, religious leaders have designed complicated rules to enforce their myths, establishing elaborate means of control, promising hope, and threatening punishment for disobedience.

Religions made sense when our world was in its pre-scientific era. Today, with the fantastic advances we have made in science, medicine, and technology – along with our greater ability to understand history – religions have become unnecessary relics preventing humanity's advancement. In short: Religions don't set us free; they weigh us down.

I hope this book has encouraged you that it *is* possible to be good without gods, and to live an ethical life filled with wisdom and compassion.

Using critical thinking we can foster curiosity rather than judgment, focus on improving the plight of all people through secular education, and build a sustainable world with equality and dignity for all. Let us look for opportunities to serve and to share, creating safe and supportive secular communities everywhere.

FINAL THOUGHTS

Divorcing Religion was one of the hardest and most painful events of my life, and I don't regret it one bit. My voyage of freedom and self-discovery has been like a shooting star, taking me higher and farther than I ever imagined. I am grateful to stand on the shoulders of religious trauma recovery giants like Dr. Marlene Winell and Dr. Darrel Ray, and I am sincerely thankful to all who support my work.

You have now reached the end of *Divorcing Religion: A Memoir and Survival Handbook*. I hope your time with me has been interesting and helpful.

I'd love to hear from you at Janice@divorcing-religion.com if:

- You found something in my book that challenged or encouraged you
- You would benefit from 1:1 religious trauma recovery coaching or counselling
- You have an interesting story to share on the Divorcing Religion podcast about your own recovery from religious trauma
- You're a mental health professional or related expert wanting to speak at CORT or the Shameless Sexuality: Life After Purity Culture conference.

ABOUT THE AUTHOR

Janice Selbie lives in British Columbia with her husband, daughter, and two cats. She is a life-long learner who is happy to share her experiences about Divorcing Religion in the hope of helping others. Her plans include continuing to provide religious trauma recovery coaching, hosting the Divorcing Religion Podcast, writing more books, and eventually doing some stand-up comedy.

www.ingramcontent.com/pod-product-compliance
Lightning Source LLC
Chambersburg PA
CBHW071649090426
42738CB00009B/1470